*A Gathering of Angels*

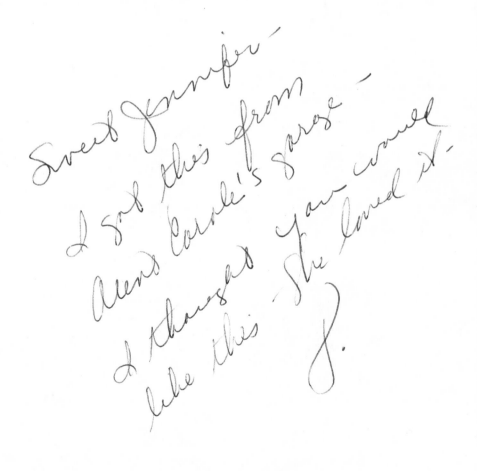

Sweet Jennifer —

I got this from
Aunt Carole's garage —
I thought you would
like this. She loved it.

J.

# A Gathering of Angels

~

MORRIS B. MARGOLIES

*Ballantine Books*
*New York*

Copyright © 1994 by Rabbi Morris B. Margolies

All rights reserved under International and Pan-American Copyright Conventions. Published in the United States by Ballantine Books, a division of Random House, Inc., New York, and simultaneously in Canada by Random House of Canada Limited, Toronto.

Grateful acknowledgment is made to the following for permission to reprint previously published material:

*Jason Aronson Inc.*: Excerpts from *The Hasidic Anthology: Tales and Teaching of the Hasidim* by Louis I. Newman. Reprinted by permission of the publisher, Jason Aronson Inc., Northvale, NJ. © 1987.

*Doubleday*: Excerpts from *The Dead Sea Scriptures* by Theodore Gaster. Copyright © 1956, 1964, 1976 by Theodore M. Gaster. Excerpts from *The Old Testament Pseudepigrapha* by James H. Charlesworth. Copyright © 1983, 1985 by James H. Charlesworth. Reprinted by permission of Doubleday, a division of Bantam Doubleday Dell Publishing Group, Inc.

*Farrar, Straus & Giroux, Inc. and Laurence Pollinger Limited*: Excerpts from "Jachid and Jechidah" and "The Last Demon" from *Short Friday and Other Stories* by Isaac Bashevis Singer. Copyright © 1964 by Isaac Bashevis Singer, renewed © 1992 by Alma Singer. Excerpts from "Shiddah and Kuziba" from *The Spinoza of Market Street* by Isaac Bashevis Singer. Copyright © 1958, 1960, 1961 by Isaac Bashevis Singer, renewed © 1989 by Isaac Bashevis Singer. Published in the British Commonwealth by Jonathan Cape Ltd. Reprinted by permission of Farrar, Straus & Giroux, Inc. and Laurence Pollinger Limited.

*Jewish Publications Society*: Excerpts from *Ma'aseh Book: Volume 1* by Moses Gaster, 1934. Excerpts from *Prince of the Ghetto* translated by Maurice Samuel, 1959. Excerpts from *The Torah*. Excerpts from *The Legends of the Jews: Volume 4* by Louis Ginsberg, 1946. Reprinted by permission of Jewish Publications Society, Philadelphia.

*Jerome Rothenberg*: Excerpt from "The Angel and the World's Dominion" reprinted from Martin Buber, *Tales of Angels, Spirits and Demons*, Hawk's Well Press, 1958, by permission of the translator, Jerome Rothenberg.

*Schocken Books Inc.*: Excerpt from *The Diaries of Franz Kafka, 1914–1923,* by Franz Kafka, translated by Martin Greenberg. Copyright 1949 and renewed 1977 by Schocken Books Inc. Excerpt from *The Correspondence of Walter Benjamin and Gershom Scholem 1932–1940* by Gershom Scholem, translated by F. Gary Smith. Copyright © 1989 by Schocken Books Inc. Reprinted by permission of Schocken Books, published by Pantheon Books, a division of Random House, Inc.

*Howard Schwartz*: Excerpts from "The Three Souls of Reb Aharon" by Howard Schwartz and "The Eden Angel" by Nachmann Rapp from *Gates to the New City*, edited by Howard Schwartz. Copyright 1983, 1991 by Howard Schwartz.

Library of Congress Catalog Card Number: 93-90473

ISBN: 0-345-38104-1

COVER DESIGN BY Kathleen Lynch

COVER PAINTING: Botticini and Verrochio. *Tre arcangeli e Tobiolo* (Firenze, Galleria Uffizi/Art Resource).

TEXT DESIGN BY: Beth Tondreau Design/Mary A. Wirth

Manufactured in the United States of America
First Edition: March 1994
10   9   8   7   6   5   4   3   2   1

*For Malka*

~

# Acknowledgments

My gratitude is owed to a number of people for their help with this project. My daughter Malka Margolies is responsible for its genesis. My daughter-in-law Diane Westover Margolies painstakingly input the manuscript into the word processor. Bertha Pener did the original typescript. My wife, Ruth, was a patient and helpful first reader, and my daughter-in-law Deborah Salkov made useful critical comments. Jill Singer was of great help in the preparation of the final copy of the text.

Last, not least, I thank my editor, Julie Merberg, for her enthusiasm and invaluable suggestions throughout the writing and rewriting of this book. I am fortunate to have had the pleasure of working with her.

MBM

~

# Contents

*An Introduction to the Sources*                3

The Hebrew Bible                                3
Apocrypha and Pseudepigrapha                    4
The Dead Sea Scrolls                            5
The Talmud                                      5
The *Zohar* and Medieval Literature             6
Elijah                                          7
Post-Holocaust Literature                       7

CHAPTER 1 ~ ~ ~ ~ ~ ~ ~ ~ ~ ~ ~ ~ ~ ~ ~
*The Angels Within Us*                          9

CHAPTER 2 ~ ~ ~ ~ ~ ~ ~ ~ ~ ~ ~ ~ ~ ~ ~
*Angels in the Hebrew Bible*                    15

The Hebrew Bible     15

The Cherubim     18

Hagar and the Angels     20

The Angel of Mount Moriah     22

The Angels on Jacob's Ladder     25

Jacob Wrestles with the Angel     29

The Angel of the Burning Bush     32

The Angel and Balaam's Ass     35

The Angels of Joshua, Gideon, and Manoah's Wife     39

The Angels of the Book of Daniel     52

CHAPTER 3 ∼∼∼∼∼∼∼∼∼∼∼∼∼∼

*Angels in the Dead Sea Scrolls Era*     60

The Scroll People     60

Pharisees, Sadducees, and Essenes     69

Apocrypha and Pseudepigrapha     76

Metatron     80

The Angelic Inner Circle     83

    Michael     83

    Tobit and Raphael     86

    Gabriel     90

    Uriel     91

CHAPTER 4 ∼∼∼∼∼∼∼∼∼∼∼∼∼∼

*Satan and His Angels*     99

The Source Material     99

Satan and Job     101

Satan and the Fallen Angels                    104
Satan and King Manasseh                        110
The Original Sin: Two Views                    112
Fear of the Angel of Death                     113
Satan's Corrupted Nature                       120
Is Satan Necessary?                            123
A Registry of Immortals                        124

CHAPTER 5    ≈ ≈ ≈ ≈ ≈ ≈ ≈ ≈ ≈ ≈ ≈ ≈ ≈ ≈
*The Rabbis and the Angels*                     128

The Talmud                                     128
Putting Angels in Their Place                  130
Argumentative Angels                           138
Walking with the Right Angels                  144

CHAPTER 6    ≈ ≈ ≈ ≈ ≈ ≈ ≈ ≈ ≈ ≈ ≈ ≈ ≈ ≈
*The Age of Demons*                             149

What Are Demons?                               149
Background and Sources                         152
Demons and History                             153
Enter Asmodeus, King of the Demons             156
Solomon and Asmodeus                           162
Lilith                                         165
    Lilith, the Queen of Sheba?                168
    Lilith Today                               172
The Dybbuk                                     173

Demons and the Kabbalah      175
Joseph della Reina and Samael      179

CHAPTER 7 ≈≈≈≈≈≈≈≈≈≈≈≈

*Angels and Hasidim*      184

Hasidim in the Age of Enlightenment      184
Angels Are Created by Humans      187
Of Humans and Angels      190
The Niggun in the Air      193
Prenatal Angels      194
"To Break Off Every Yoke"      195
Out of the Fire      197

CHAPTER 8 ≈≈≈≈≈≈≈≈≈≈≈≈

*Elijah, the Prophet-Angel*      200

Elijah, the Living Legend      200
Elijah and Ahab      203
Elijah the Zealot      205
Elijah Transported      210
The Heavenly Elijah      211
God's Helping Hand      214
Redressing Injustice      215
Elijah and the Messiah      217

CHAPTER 9 ⩘ ⩘ ⩘ ⩘ ⩘ ⩘ ⩘ ⩘ ⩘ ⩘ ⩘ ⩘ ⩘ ⩘ ⩘
*Angels in Jewish Prayers* 221

Evolution of the Jewish Liturgy 221
The Role of Angels in Jewish Prayer 223
Prayers as Angels 231

CHAPTER 10 ⩘ ⩘ ⩘ ⩘ ⩘ ⩘ ⩘ ⩘ ⩘ ⩘ ⩘ ⩘ ⩘ ⩘
*Angels in Modern Dress* 233

Angels Today? 233
Steinsaltz's Angels 234
The Elusive Angel 236
Angel of Light 240
The Thirty-six Righteous 243
The Demons of Isaac Bashevis Singer 249

CHAPTER 11 ⩘ ⩘ ⩘ ⩘ ⩘ ⩘ ⩘ ⩘ ⩘ ⩘ ⩘ ⩘ ⩘ ⩘
*The Last Words* 258

Endnotes 264
Bibliography 268

*A Gathering of Angels*

*~*

*An*

*Introduction*

*to the*

*Sources*

## *The Hebrew Bible* (*1000* B.C.E.–*100* C.E.)

∾ ∾ ∾ ∾ ∾ ∾ ∾ ∾ ∾ ∾ ∾ ∾ ∾ ∾ ∾ ∾ ∾ ∾ ∾ ∾ ∾ ∾ ∾

A ngels are an ancient element in Jewish tradition, first appearing in the earliest passages of the Hebrew Bible (The Old Testament), which date back some three thousand years. Then they pop up sporadically throughout the Bible, which was compiled over a period of a thousand years and edited by the Rabbis after the middle of the first century as the authorized Holy Scriptures.

Scores of books dealing with religious themes had been circulating among the Jews at the time, though most were excluded from the canon by the Rabbis. The books left out of the Bible are designated as the Apocrypha ("outside writings") and the Pseudepigrapha (writings attributed by the author to someone else, usually a well-known biblical character such as Enoch, Ezra, or Elijah).

## Apocrypha and Pseudepigrapha (200 B.C.E.–100 C.E.)

The works comprising the Apocrypha and Pseudepigrapha were composed over a period of nearly three hundred years—from roughly 200 B.C.E. to 100 C.E., years of severe crises for the Jewish people. The quest for supernatural redemption from suffering is reflected in this literature, and angels suddenly fill virtually every page. While the Rabbis stopped short of denying the existence of angels, they felt compelled to censor a literature in which angels seem to be autonomous. The Judaic first principle that God is one is in jeopardy when He is buttressed by so much celestial assistance. So, the Rabbis instituted the virtual disappearance of the Apocrypha-Pseudepigrapha from Jewish literature.

On the other hand, Christianity, which was born during this period, incorporated many of these writings into its own version of Holy Scripture, assuring their survival.

## The Dead Sea Scrolls (c. 200 B.C.E.–100 C.E.)

≈ ≈ ≈ ≈ ≈ ≈ ≈ ≈ ≈ ≈ ≈ ≈ ≈ ≈ ≈ ≈ ≈ ≈ ≈ ≈ ≈

The discovery of the Dead Sea Scrolls in 1947 brightly illuminated the period of these writings. Though the Scroll people (probably the Essene sect) developed their own notions of angelology, there is an unmistakable kinship between the Dead Sea Scrolls and the Apocrypha-Pseudepigrapha, especially in regard to apocalyptic visions and hopes, and angels play a crucial role for both.

## The Talmud (200–500 C.E.)

≈ ≈ ≈ ≈ ≈ ≈ ≈ ≈ ≈ ≈ ≈ ≈ ≈ ≈ ≈ ≈ ≈ ≈ ≈ ≈ ≈

With the destruction of the Second Temple by the Romans in the year 70, the survival of the Jewish people was underwritten by the great Rabbis who encoded Jewish law and belief over the course of the next five hundred years, ultimately producing the Talmud. This immense opus became the guiding light of Judaism to the present day. The Talmud's position on angels is of the utmost importance if we are to understand the role angels play in the Jewish mind. The thousands of homilies or sermons that are scattered throughout the Talmud and are known collectively as Midrash (inquiry into the biblical texts) help to illustrate the Talmud's position on specific issues. And it is in the Talmud that the basic structure of Jewish liturgy is outlined. The arrival, existence, and position of angels in the context of prayer are all considered in this liturgy.

## The Zohar and Medieval Literature (Thirteenth century C.E.)

The mystic trend in Judaism can be traced back over a period of two thousand years, but it was not until the thirteenth century that the classic work of Jewish mysticism, the *Zohar*, was published. From then on, Kabbalah, the mystic tradition in Judaism, loomed large in the beliefs of an increasing number of Jews, and the writings of the Kabbalah featured angels and devils in idiosyncratic roles.

Shortly before the *Zohar* was published, a pietistic movement emerged in Germany under the leadership of Rabbi Judah the Pious. Its exalted level of morality was accompanied by deep-seated superstitious beliefs in devils, imps, demons, and their ilk, and Jewish medieval folklore is filled with tales about these creatures as well as magical formulae with which to dominate them.

## Elijah (Ninth century B.C.E.)

≈ ≈ ≈ ≈ ≈ ≈ ≈ ≈ ≈ ≈ ≈ ≈ ≈ ≈ ≈ ≈ ≈ ≈ ≈ ≈ ≈ ≈

The prophet Elijah occupies a special place in Jewish angelic lore. Elijah lived in Israel during the ninth pre-Christian century and—having been taken to heaven in a chariot of fire drawn by fiery horses—became the most popular, most written about of all angels. Elijah legends are found in the Talmud, the several compilations of Midrash, and in medieval literature, most prominently in the twelfth-century *Sefer Hasidim* and in the *Zohar*.

## Post-Holocaust Literature (Twentieth century)

≈ ≈ ≈ ≈ ≈ ≈ ≈ ≈ ≈ ≈ ≈ ≈ ≈ ≈ ≈ ≈ ≈ ≈ ≈ ≈ ≈ ≈

Modern Jewish thinkers and writers underscore the continuing need for supernatural images in parable and metaphor. In light of the most demonic horror in human history—the systematic incineration of six million Jews by the Nazis and their collaborators—special attention is given in this book to the demons in the stories of Isaac Bashevis Singer.

In addition to the Judaic writings cited, references are made to Shakespeare, Freud, and others who touch upon similar themes. Though angels and devils hold a significant place in the Jewish tradition, the concepts they represent are universal.

CHAPTER 1

*The*

*Angels*

*Within*

*Us*

≈ ≈ ≈ ≈ ≈ ≈ ≈ ≈ ≈ ≈ ≈ ≈ ≈ ≈ ≈ ≈ ≈ ≈ ≈ ≈ ≈ ≈ ≈ ≈

I remember my mother's outcry as she scurried to lift me up when I was a child of four and had stumbled over a rock: "May the good angels be with you!" I also remember my father's outraged words another time, a year or so later, when I accidentally shattered his favorite glass ashtray: "That boy is an angel of destruction." But more pleasing to my childish ears were the words of my first schoolteacher, who told both of my parents: "Moishe'le your son? Why Moishe'le is a *malakh*!" *Malakh* is the Hebrew-Yiddish word for angel. When used without qualifiers it means good and noble, helpful and sweet. I was, in fact, none of the above. But I *was* a learner, and the value of these rather ordinary experiences is that my fascination with angels began early in my life.

As I grew up, my angels changed: Their cherubic faces and indispensable wings faded as their essence and significance grew in my mind. As I read more of the angelogical lore in the Jewish literature—from the Bible through Kabbalah to the teachings of the Hasidic masters—it became ever more clear to me that angels are better understood as symbols of forces that operate within every one of us. Some are forces for good, some for evil; some are healing and protective, some destructive.

Angels are metaphors for the most basic human drives and emotions: love, hate, envy, lust, charity, malice, greed, generosity, sadism, delusion, vision, despair, fear, and hope. "The gathering of angels" set in heaven by John Milton is placed right here on earth by Jewish teaching. That gathering is within each one of us.

This interpretation of angels reconciles their existence with the teachings of a monotheistic faith. The most essential Jewish credo is: "Hear, O Israel, the Lord our God, the Lord is *One*." The One shares His sovereignty with no other. The One needs help from no other. So does such a One need angels? Are angels not, in fact, blasphemy to the conception of one God?

If we view angels as parts of our own beings, we affirm that God needs no angels—but we mortals do. Moreover, having angels within us helps narrow the vast chasm that separates us from God. Angels become aspects of being to whom we can relate. Strictly speaking, as the great master Moses Maimonides (1135–1204 C.E.) put it, *no* adjective is applicable to God if it describes physical phenomena. But words drawn from our human experience *can* be transferred to angels, and to that extent our lives begin to touch God and to be touched by Him in ways that render faith more concrete.

Still, the master teachers of the Talmud sensed the danger inherent in the acceptance of angels: Angels could become objects of adoration, worship, and prayer, and God's One-ness could be seriously threatened. The Rabbis of the Talmud fought this danger in a variety of ways. One law decreed: "Whoever offers sacrifices to the Archangel Michael indulges in idolatry." And Rabbi Yudan, a fourth-century Palestinian, offered this explanation: "Human beings have their patrons. In time of trouble a person does not crash into the home of his patron without being announced. Rather he stands by the entrance of the patron and speaks to the servant or doorman petitioning admittance. Not so is it with the Holy One, Blessed be He. Should a person be in trouble he is not to plead with Michael or with Gabriel. He is to call upon God directly and will receive immediate response." Over and over, Jewish teaching stresses that angels are not independent powers, rather, they are the agents of God. Even Satan, a fallen angel, is dependent upon the will of God. He couldn't touch Job without divine permission. He couldn't impose famine upon King David and his people without God's sanction. And Satan could not have lured Eve and Adam into sin without divine license to do so.

It has always been problematic, though, to speak of the One God as creator of evil. Why would an all-powerful God allow evil to exist if He is also—as is claimed by Jewish tradition—all-merciful? This is the most troubling of all theological questions. The Book of Job, arguably the masterpiece of the Bible, is devoted entirely to a consideration of this question. Job, the just and the good, sustains a series of calamities, all inflicted upon him by Satan—with God's permission. Job, shattered in body but not in spirit, eventually dares to question God's justice, ultimately denying the premise that God is just and good. Though God finally does respond to Job in what are some of the most sublime passages in the Hebrew Bible, His answer falls far short of addressing why bad things happen to good people. The sensitive reader of the Book of Job cannot fail to be awed and inspired, but ultimately frustrated.

There are many explanations—none really satisfying. We do believe that some perverse entity like a Satan is somehow involved, even if Satan is subject to God's will and purpose. Perhaps that purpose is to underscore the presence—and hopefully the dominance—of good; perhaps we are meant to fear, and to fight evil on our own. We are constantly forced to choose for ourselves, which puts us in control of our lives.

THE DEVIL ASSUMES many guises in Judaic literature, the common denominator being his design to seduce, tempt, and entrap. Like angels who do good, the devil or Satan is also a metaphor for aspects of our own nature.

Mercy *and* savagery are inherent in every human being. Jewish lore from biblical times to our own day utilizes angels and devils to dramatize this essential truth. Life on earth is an unending confrontation within ourselves between the best and the worst of us, between the angelic and the satanic. What will prevail in the end? That question remains a crucial concern in the biblical narratives dealing with the complexity of human nature.

The fact that devils—or evil—are just as much a part of us and of the world as are angels and goodness naturally sets limits on human potential—and, in a way, on an all-powerful, all-merciful God. Perhaps God allows the presence of evil so that, like Job, we can test the power of good, the strength of our angels. Perhaps He wants us to appreciate rather than expect these forces of good, and by placing the angels within us, He enables us to shape our own worlds.

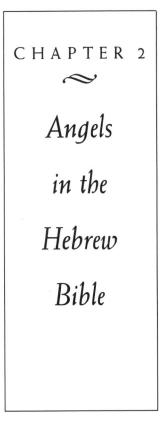

CHAPTER 2

*Angels*

*in the*

*Hebrew*

*Bible*

## *The Hebrew Bible*

The Hebrew Bible—the *Tanakh*—is the canonized religious literature of the Jews. It was composed and transmitted over a span of one thousand years, from about

1250 B.C.E. to about 200 B.C.E. In its present form, edited by the Rabbis of the second century in Palestine, it includes twenty-four books divided into three sections: Torah, Prophets, and Writings. The Torah contains the Books of Genesis, Exodus, Leviticus, Numbers, and Deuteronomy, also called the Five Books of Moses.

Genesis begins with the creation of the universe and ends with the enslavement in Egypt of the Children of Israel. Its main protagonists are Adam and Eve, Noah, Abraham, Isaac, Jacob, and Joseph.

Exodus narrates the redemption of the Children of Israel from Egypt at the hands of Moses and closes with their wandering through the wilderness. Exodus also includes the first codes of Judaic law.

Leviticus is mainly a manual to guide the priests through the various rituals of the Tabernacle in the wilderness. It also outlines priestly law for the generations to follow.

Then Numbers describes the further adventures of the Israelites in the Sinai wilderness and gives a detailed military table of organization for the twelve tribes of Israel.

Finally, Deuteronomy consists of three major orations given by Moses to his people just prior to his death at the borders of the Promised Land. In addition to these discourses, the book contains Moses' epic poem on the destiny of his people, as well as his verses of blessing for each of the tribes.

The beautifully written narrative books of the second section, the Prophets, span the period of about 1200 B.C.E.

to the year 539 B.C.E. Prophets begins with the Israelites'
conquest of Canaan and ends with their exile to Babylonia
in 586 B.C.E. Conspicuous among its protagonists are
Joshua, Gideon, Samson, David, Solomon, Ahab, Elijah,
Nebuchadnezzar, Zerubbabel, and Obadiah, who will all
be discovered later.

The teaching of the Prophets is the lifeblood of Judaism,
incorporating its noblest ideals and aspirations. Within this
section, the Prophets constantly assert the One-ness of God
and relegate angels to the role of divine agents or messengers.

The third and final section of the Hebrew Bible, the
Writings, contains some narrative material, most notably
in the Books of Ezra-Nehemiah, Ruth, Esther, and Chronicles. The larger part of the section includes the books of
Psalms, Proverbs, Job, and Daniel. The last two bear special importance to this work: Satan makes his most dramatic biblical appearance in Job, and the names of angels
are given for the first time in Daniel. While the date of the
composition of the Book of Job is still a point of contention
among scholars, the writing of the Book of Daniel can be
dated almost precisely to the years 170–160 B.C.E., the period of the Maccabean Revolt against pagan Hellenism, the
civilization of the Greek world.

≈ ≈ ≈

# The Cherubim

~ ~ ~ ~ ~ ~ ~ ~ ~ ~ ~ ~ ~ ~ ~ ~ ~ ~ ~ ~ ~ ~ ~ ~ ~ ~

The cherubim are a form of angels, the first angels to appear in the Bible. Though we think of cherubim as being cheerful, our first encounter with them in Genesis marks the culmination of Adam and Eve's fall from grace and their expulsion from paradise.

After Adam and Eve, lured by the serpent, ate of the forbidden tree, God banished them and He "stationed east of the garden of Eden the cherubim and the fiery ever-turning sword, to guard the way to the tree of life." (Genesis 3)

The cherubim are divine beings in God's inner circle according to the prophets Isaiah and Ezekiel, among others. The serpent is also identified as an angel—the Angel of Death—or as Satan, Samael, and the *Yetzer ha-Ra*, the inborn evil inclination of every human being. This is constantly in conflict with the *Yetzer-tov*, the inborn inclination to do good.

This last serpentine identification unlocks the key to the metaphor of angels (and the devil) in the Jewish tradition. The serpent is always *within* us: temptation to commit self-destructive acts. God also gave man the capacity to resist temptation, to thwart evil, and to do good. As we know, the tree of knowledge represents both good and evil, for knowledge can heal as well as destroy. Man was "created in God's image" in the sense that he was endowed with the intelligence necessary to distinguish between good and evil and so to act accordingly. Should man's destructive tendencies (Freud's *mortido*) prevail over his creative impulses (Freud's *libido*), the cherubim become angels of destruction. The "ever-turning sword" can sway in either direction.

My first schoolteacher provided his eight-year-old students with a commentary on this passage that I remember to this day. He compared us to innocents in the Garden of Eden, and assured us we would not be responsible for our actions—even if we misbehaved—until we were bar-mitsvah at the age of thirteen. But he warned us that after we became adults under Jewish law, every one of our sins would create a devil or demon who would hound us at every turn. The serpents who would frighten us would be serpents of our own making, and they would poison our lives. On the other hand, he insisted that each of our good deeds would create a guardian angel at our sides to take us through fires and storms and sickness and heartache. The more good deeds, the more guardian angels. He was teaching us, at a very early age, that we create our own company, a very sophisticated lesson that has held up well over the many years of thought I've given the subject.

≈ ≈ ≈

*Hagar and Ishmael*

## Hagar and the Angels

〜〜〜〜〜〜〜〜〜〜〜〜〜〜〜〜〜〜〜〜〜〜〜〜〜〜

On two separate occasions, abused and expelled by her mistress, Sarah (wife of Abraham), the Egyptian maid-servant Hagar found herself at her wit's end, without hope. On the first such occasion, Hagar was heavy with Abra-

ham's child and Sarah sent her out into the wilderness to fend
for herself. She was alone, in pain, at the border of despair.

> An angel of the Lord found her by a spring of water in the
> wilderness and said: "Hagar, slave of Sarai, where have you
> come from, and where are you going?" And she said, "I am
> running away from my mistress Sarai."
>
> And the angel of the Lord said to her, "Go back to your
> mistress, and submit to her harsh treatment. I will greatly
> increase your offspring. And they shall be too many to
> count . . . Behold, you are with child and shall bear a son;
> you shall call him Ishmael, for the Lord has paid heed to
> your suffering." (GENESIS 16:7–11)

Hagar's angel showed her the vision of a brighter tomor-
row, if only she could summon enough hope to survive her
day of darkness. So she went back to endure and gave birth
to Ishmael, Abraham's first son. Sarai-Sarah was still childless and could not bear what she took to be a show of superiority in her maidservant Hagar. So once again Sarah
persuaded a very reluctant Abraham to exile Hagar along
with the infant Ishmael.

> Early next morning Abraham took some bread and a skin
> of water, and gave them to Hagar . . . And she wandered
> about in the wilderness of Beer-sheba. When the water was
> gone from the skin, she left the child under one of the
> bushes, and went and sat down at a distance . . . for she
> thought, "Let me not look on as the child dies." And sitting
> thus afar, she burst into tears. (GENESIS 21:14–16)

The master poet of Genesis offers a moving portrait of heartbreak. Then, through her tears, Hagar sees an angel of God, who says:

> "What troubles you, Hagar. Fear not, for God has heeded the cry of the boy . . . Come, lift up the boy and hold him by the hand, for I will make a great nation of him."
>
> (GENESIS 21:17, 18)

In both of these celestial encounters, nothing miraculous is performed by the angel. Instead, on each occasion the angel calls upon Hagar to help herself. Good angels reside within the human heart—if that heart is hospitable to them.

## The Angel of Mount Moriah

≈≈≈≈≈≈≈≈≈≈≈≈≈≈≈≈≈≈≈≈≈≈≈

The birth of Isaac—son of ninety-year-old Sarah and Abraham, the centenarian—was surely a miracle. Sarah, amazed, said: "God has brought me laughter; everyone who hears will laugh with me . . . Who would have said to Abraham that Sarah would suckle children! Yet I have borne a son in his old age." Isaac was truly a dream come true. For all their married lives, Sarah and Abraham prayed and yearned for the child. Finally, Isaac was born to unbounded joy. And then came the real test of faith when God commanded Abraham to offer this favorite son as a burnt offering.

In perplexing, unquestioning submission, Abraham took Isaac to the designated spot. After laying out the wood, Abraham bound Isaac and placed him on the altar, over the wood. Then, when he picked up the knife to actually slay his son, he was interrupted:

> Then an angel of the Lord called to him from heaven: "Abraham! Abraham . . . Do not raise your hand against the boy . . . For now I know that you fear God, since you have not withheld your son, your favored one from Me." . . . And Abraham named that site Adonai-Yireh (the Lord will see). Whence the present saying: "On the mount of the Lord there is vision."
>
> (GENESIS 22:11–14)

The mistitled "Sacrifice of Isaac" (in the Christian tradition; the Jewish title is *"Akedat Yitzhak,"* or "The Binding of Isaac") has been the subject of much literature, theology, mysticism, and art. It is high drama, to say the very least. It is also puzzling and infuriating, and it puts both Abraham and God in a bad light.

The message of the angel of the Lord from heaven offers the key to understanding what the Mount of Moriah was about. The angel's message was essentially that God wants no killing done in His name. This was a far cry from the

*The Trial of Abraham's Faith*

practices Abraham had seen previously in the pagan world, where sacrifice was a display of total faith. Withholding the sword of violence is the way Abraham's faith was ultimately vindicated. This significant lesson, which would become a tenet of Judaism, was first conveyed by an angel.

## The Angels on Jacob's Ladder

≋ ≋ ≋ ≋ ≋ ≋ ≋ ≋ ≋ ≋ ≋ ≋ ≋ ≋ ≋ ≋ ≋ ≋ ≋

Well before Freud, as far back as two thousand years ago, the ancient Rabbis believed that dreams were nocturnal reflections of daytime obsessions, both conscious and subconscious. While many dreams are recounted in the Hebrew Bible, it's interesting that most biblical tales of human encounters with angels are dream sequences, even when the text does not say so. The angels on Jacob's ladder explicitly appear to him in a dream.

Because of the wrath and jealousy of his twin brother, Esau, Jacob was forced into exile, leaving his parents, Rebecca and Isaac, his native land of Canaan, and all that he had grown to cherish.

> Jacob left Beer-sheba and set out for Haran. He came upon a certain place and stopped there for the night, for the sun had set. Taking one of the stones of that place, he put it under his head and lay down there. He had a dream; a ladder was set on the ground and its top reached to the sky,

and angels of God were going up and down on it. And the Lord was standing beside him and He said, "I am the Lord, the God of your father Abraham and the God of Isaac . . . Remember, I am with you: I will protect you wherever you go and will bring you back to this land. I will not leave you until I have done what I have promised you.

Jacob awoke from his sleep and said: "Surely the Lord is present in this place and I did not know it! . . . How awesome is this place! This is none other than the abode of God, and that is the gateway to heaven."

(GENESIS 28:10–17)

The angels of God were going up and down the ladder, a seemingly meaningless exercise. They don't even say a word to the dreaming Jacob: It is God who does all the talking.

The angels ascending and descending is at the core of Jacob's vision, telling him that life is two-directional. Its valleys are as normal as its peaks, its defeats as frequent as its triumphs. In this light, exile can be seen as the prelude to going home again—if you have faith that God is by your side wherever you are, and that even when you hit the bottom rung of the ladder you are still in the company of angels.

This sentiment is echoed in the Ninety-first Psalm:

You shall not be afraid of the terror by night, nor of the arrow that flies by day; of the pestilence that stalks in darkness, nor of the destruction that ravages at noonday . . .

*Jacob's Dream*

there shall no evil befall you, nor any scourge come near your tent. For He will charge His angels to watch over you wherever you go.

(PSALMS 91:5-11)

IN THE SPRING OF 1492, Their Royal Highnesses of Castile and Aragon, Isabella and Ferdinand, gave the Jews of Spain three months to either accept the Catholic faith or get out of the country. Jews had lived on the Iberian Peninsula for well over a thousand years and had contributed mightily to Spain's cultural, economic, and political prosperity. Even when they had been massacred in the thousands by religious fanatics in 1391, most Jews chose to remain, despite the Inquisition and persecutions. But in 1492 over 150,000 Jews chose exile over the betrayal of their millennial faith. As the ships of Christopher Columbus passed the Straits of Gibraltar on their way to the New World, the admiral reported in his diary the sight of rotted ships with their miserable cargo of Jews forced out of their homes and headed for uncertain havens.

Among them was Don Isaac Abravanel, who had faithfully and brilliantly served the financial affairs of both Aragon and Castile. He was one of the most distinguished Jews of Spanish history. A man of fine business acumen, he was at the same time a profound scholar and thinker. He was fifty-five years old at the time of the expulsion and lived elsewhere in Europe for another fifteen years. During those

years he wrote great commentaries on the Bible and trea-
tises saturated with deep religious faith. In one of his commentaries, Abravanel declares that the angels of Jacob's
ladder were with his people in their agony but that he had
no doubt that they would ascend to heaven's gateway
along with their ascending guardian angels. He was opti-
mist enough to believe that this would happen in his own
lifetime, though it took about 450 years longer. There are
streets in Jerusalem, Tel Aviv, Haifa, and other places in
Israel bearing Abravanel's name. Perhaps Don Isaac and
his angels dwell there today.

## Jacob Wrestles with the Angel

During his twenty years in Mesopotamia, Jacob toiled
day and night for his ruthless and demanding father-
in-law, Laban. There he married Leah and Rachel and sired
eleven sons and one daughter (Benjamin was to be born
later near Bethlehem, where his mother, Rachel, died in
childbirth). When Jacob finally decided to return to his native Canaan, he heard that his brother, Esau, was coming
to meet him with an army of four hundred men. (Esau felt
that Jacob, the younger but favorite son of Isaac, had un-
fairly taken the birthright.) Jacob was greatly frightened,
and he prayed:

"O God of my father Abraham and God of my father Isaac, O Lord, who said to me, 'Return to your native land and I will deal bountifully with you.' I am unworthy of all the kindness that you have so steadfastly shown Your servant: with my staff alone I crossed this Jordan and now I have become two camps. Deliver me, I pray, from the hand of my brother, from the hand of Esau; else, I fear, he may come and strike me down, mothers and children alike. Yet You have said, 'I will deal kindly with you and make your off-spring as the sands of the sea, which are too numerous to count.' "

(GENESIS 32:10–13)

That night, Jacob transported his family and flocks across the stream Jabbok.

Jacob was left alone. And a man wrestled with him until the break of dawn. When he saw that he had not prevailed against him, he wrenched Jacob's hip at its socket, so that the socket of his hip was strained as he wrestled with him. Then he said, "Let me go, for dawn is breaking." But he answered, "I will not let you go unless you bless me." Said the other, "What is your name?" He replied, "Jacob." Said he, "Your name shall no longer be Jacob, but Israel, for you have striven with beings divine and human and have prevailed." Jacob asked, "Pray tell me your name." But he said: "You must not ask my name!" And he took leave of him there.

(GENESIS 32:25–30)

*Jacob Wrestling with the Angel*

Early rabbinic literature identified the angel (clearly, this divine being was an angel) as none other than the Archangel Gabriel—a fitting opponent for Jacob's wrestling match. Jacob, fearing the potential disaster he would face at daybreak, needed the quality of courage at this crossroads of Jabbok—and Gabriel was there to supply it. He was, in effect, a sparring partner helping to prepare a fighter for the main event, and Jacob fought bravely against superior force. He wrestled with the angel whose very name is synonymous with *Gvurah*, the Hebrew word for "power," continuing in mortal combat even when he was sorely wounded. And Jacob prevailed.

He sought a blessing as the prize, and Gabriel responded that he had earned a new name, that of Israel, which means "he *will* contend with the mighty"—with the courage born of conviction and of faith. The name Jacob, meaning "hanger on," no longer suited him. He had come of age, and Gabriel renamed him Israel.

## The Angel of the Burning Bush

Jacob's children and grandchildren—a family of seventy in all—were obliged by a famine to leave their land of Canaan and to make their temporary home in Egypt, where food was available. Their stay in Egypt proved to be extended and traumatic. They were enslaved by later Pharaohs.

But the more they were oppressed, the more they increased and spread out . . . The Egyptians ruthlessly imposed upon the Israelites the various labors that they had made them perform. They made life bitter for them with harsh labor at mortar and bricks and with all sorts of tasks in the field.

(EXODUS 1:12–14)

This was followed by the brutal edict of drowning every newborn Israelite male in the Nile River. One Hebrew child named Moses survived, grew to manhood, and took up the battle on behalf of his oppressed people. Early in his career, Moses killed an Egyptian, was forced to escape to Midian, and eventually married a Midianite woman and became shepherd of the flock of his father-in-law, Jethro.

But Moses' restless imagination gave him no respite and his dreams of Israelite emancipation allowed him only turbulent sleep. One of the most stunning chapters of the Hebrew Bible, the third chapter of the Book of Exodus, begins as follows:

Now Moses, tending the flock of his father-in-law Jethro, the Priest of Midian, drove the flock into the wilderness, and came to Horeb, the Mountain of God. An angel of the Lord appeared to him in a blazing fire out of a bush. He gazed, and there was a bush all aflame, yet the bush was not consumed. Moses said, "I must turn aside to look at this marvelous sight; why doesn't the bush burn up?" When the Lord saw that he had turned aside to look, God called to him out of the bush: "Moses! Moses!" He answered: "Here

I am." And He said: "Do not come closer. Remove your sandals from your feet, for the place on which you stand is holy ground. I am . . . the God of your father, the God of Abraham, the God of Isaac, and the God of Jacob . . . I have marked well the plight of My people in Egypt . . . I am mindful of their sufferings . . . Come, therefore, I will send you to Pharaoh, and you shall free My people, the Israelites, from Egypt."

(EXODUS 3:1–10)

Though "an angel of the Lord" appeared to Moses in the burning bush, God Himself spoke to Moses and gave him His momentous charge. So this passage underscores the rigidly monotheistic faith that is born at the very site of the burning bush—God is invisible and intangible. The *voice* of God may be heard by those whom He has chosen, but God Himself can never be seen, not even by Moses. So the angel of the burning bush is the spiritual entity who appears to Moses, drawing his attention to the voice of God.

This angel—like the angel who appeared to Hagar and her child, Ishmael, to signal a well of water in the desert—typifies the role of angels in the Jewish tradition.

The incident at the burning bush opened Moses' eyes to the reality of his people's remarkable experience in Egypt: enslaved, tortured, slaughtered, humiliated for centuries, they remained nevertheless alive and thriving. It was Israel in Egypt that was the burning bush "all aflame but not consumed." Such a bush had to be transplanted to terrain of its own, the land walked by the patriarchs, Abraham, Isaac, and Jacob—the land of Israel.

So Moses returned to Egypt, and shortly thereafter came the Exodus.

## The Angel and Balaam's Ass

~ ~ ~ ~ ~ ~ ~ ~ ~ ~ ~ ~ ~ ~ ~ ~ ~ ~ ~ ~ ~

The angel as "eye-opener" is dramatically depicted in the twenty-second, twenty-third, and twenty-fourth chapters of the Book of Numbers: The people of Israel, under the leadership of Moses, crossed the Red Sea, overcame many natural and military obstacles in their journeys through the Sinai Desert, and in the process greatly expanded in numbers. To Balak, King of Moab, they appeared as a formidable potential enemy who had to be stopped before it was too late.

In neighboring Pethor lived Balaam, a sort of witch doctor and seer renowned for the efficacy of his curses. Balak sent for him to pronounce a curse upon the Israelites where they were camped in the wilderness, making an offer he thought Balaam wouldn't refuse. After much hesitation, resulting from Balaam's fear of Jehovah, God of Israel, he finally consented because that very God, in a dream, gave sanction to Balaam's trip.

He was riding on his she-ass, with his two servants along-side, when the ass caught sight of the angel of the Lord standing in the way, with his drawn sword in his hand. The ass swerved from the road and went into the fields; and Balaam beat the ass to turn her back onto the road. The angel of the Lord then stationed himself in a lane between the vineyards, with a fence on either side. The ass, seeing the angel of the Lord, pressed herself against the wall and squeezed Balaam's foot against the wall; so he beat her again. Once more the angel of the Lord moved forward and stationed himself on a spot so narrow that there was no room to swerve right or left. When the ass now saw the angel of the Lord, she lay down under Balaam; and Balaam was furious and beat the ass with his stick . . .

Then the Lord uncovered Balaam's eyes, and he saw the angel of the Lord standing in the way, his drawn sword in his hand; thereupon he bowed right to the ground . . . The angel of the Lord said to Balaam, "Go with the men. But you must say nothing except what I tell you."

(NUMBERS 22:22–35)

Here is another puzzling angel episode in which a dumb animal, an *ass*, saw what the seer could not! The ass took several untoward detours, not to mention several brutal beatings, before Balaam's eyes were opened so *he* could see the angel and get his message. What's all *that* about?

The ass is the apotheosis of Balaam himself and of most people in that it is a creature of habit, lacking in imagination. What a task it must be to open the eyes of an ass!

*The Angel Appearing to Balaam*

Thinking for ourselves, like the ass choosing its own path instead of that of its rider, is the most daunting task of all.

Balaam came with his prejudices to curse the people of Israel. But when he saw them as they really were, he blessed them instead.

Balaam represents that rarest of individuals who will not permit preconceptions to obscure the truth, once the truth emerges to his sight. A prophet of paganism and sorcery, he witnessed a new phenomenon: a people who could not be cursed because it rejected the very concept of "witchcraft" as a means of exercising the will of a deity. Israel's monotheism did not accept interference with the divine purpose. A converted Balaam wondered:

> "How shall I curse,
> Whom God has not cursed
> How shall I execrate,
> Whom God has not execrated."
> (NUMBERS 23:8)

Overcome by his new ability to see what he could not or would not see before, Balaam wanted a complete identification with the people he had set out to destroy. He took up his parable and said:

> "The saying of Balaam, the son of Peor,
> And the saying of the man whose eye is opened;
> The saying of him who heareth the words of God,

Who seeth the vision of the Almighty,
Fallen down yet with opened eyes.
How beautiful are your tents of Jacob,
Your dwellings, O Israel."

(NUMBERS 24:3–5)

His eyes were opened by an angel.

# The Angels of Joshua, Gideon, and Manoah's Wife

The children of Israel finally reached the Promised Land after a forty-year journey in the wilderness. Moses arrived at its borders, but God denied him entrance. He died on the alien soil of Moab, and God Himself attended to the burial.

> Moses was a hundred and twenty years old when he died; his eyes were undimmed and his vigor unabated. And the Israelites bewailed Moses in the steppes of Moab for thirty days.
>
> The period of wailing and mourning for Moses came to an end. Now Joshua son of Nun was filled with the spirit of wisdom because Moses had laid his hands upon him; and the Israelites heeded him, doing as the Lord had commanded Moses.
>
> Never again did there arise in Israel a prophet like Moses —whom the Lord singled out, face to face, for the various signs and portents that the Lord sent him to display in the

land of Egypt, against Pharaoh and all his courtiers and his whole country, and for all the great might and awesome power that Moses displayed before all Israel.

(DEUTERONOMY 34:7-12)

These are the last lines of the Torah, or the Pentateuch, frequently described as the Five Books of Moses.

Joshua was overwhelmed by the thought of succeeding Moses and had to be reminded again and again to "be strong and resolute," Moses' advice to him. But ultimately, Joshua's confidence had to come from within himself, from his own angel. He couldn't even begin the daunting task of the conquest of Canaan without a personal encounter with that angel.

It happened when Joshua was near Jericho, he looked up and saw a man standing before him, drawn sword in hand. Joshua went up to him and asked him: "Are you one of us or our enemies?" He replied, "No, I am captain of the Lord's host. I have just arrived." Joshua threw himself face to the ground, and, prostrating himself, said to him, "What does my Lord command his servant?" The captain of the Lord's host answered Joshua, "Remove your sandals from your feet, for the place where you stand is holy." And Joshua did so.

(JOSHUA 5:13-15)

Joshua had a vision of an angel disguised as a man, as is often the case in the Hebrew Bible. Three angels appeared to Abraham in the form of humans. Jacob wrestled with a man who turned out to be an angel. Gideon's angel and the angel who appeared to Manoah's wife were in the guise of men, as we shall soon see. These and other such instances in the Hebrew Bible underscore the concept of an angel as part of man's own imagination. The angels with whom we occasionally commune come from within ourselves and it's even possible for each of us, through an act of supreme will or faith, to bring them forth when they're most needed. In a deeper sense, Joshua summoned his own angel to fortify his spirits before the inaugural battle of Jericho. A faithful disciple of Moses, Joshua well remembered that his master had been ordered to remove his sandals forty years before in very similar circumstances. At the vision of the burning bush Moses received the charge to emancipate the Israelites from the slavery of Egypt. And before the thick walls of Jericho, Joshua was given his mission to conquer the Land of Promise.

BUT THE PEOPLES of Canaan were not to be so easily displaced. Joshua died after an illustrious military career, though large areas of the land remained under the dominion of Canaanites, Jebusites, Amorites, Moabites, Midianites, Philistines, and others. The twelve tribes of Israel were frequently at odds with one another. Their consolidation into one nation was still two centuries away. In the

*The Angel Appearing to Joshua*

interim they were often victims of raids, sorties, and organized military operations of the surrounding enemies. In times of severe peril, charismatic leaders would emerge to organize enough military force and marshal sufficient spirit to repel the enemy. The Book of Judges is largely the account of such leaders—from Othniel through Samson. Their indispensable services to their people enabled the Children of Israel to maintain their foothold in Canaan until the consolidation of the nation under its first two kings—Saul and David.

Of all the Judges, my favorite is Gideon, of the tiniest of the tribes, the tribe of Manassah. Gideon sought neither power nor glory. He was a simple, hardworking farmer who was deeply affected by the harassment of his people at the hands of marauding Midianites—camel-riding bedouin who preyed upon the crops grown by Israelite farmers. He was a skeptic with a very logical turn of mind, and he, too, had an important encounter with an angel.

An angel of the Lord came and sat under the terebinth at Ophra, which belonged to Joash the Abiezrite. His son Gideon was then beating out wheat inside a winepress in order to keep it safe from the Midianites. The angel of the Lord appeared to him and said: "The Lord is with you, valiant warrior!" Gideon said to him, "Please, my Lord, if the Lord is with us, why has all this befallen us? Where are all His wondrous deeds about which our fathers told us, saying, 'Truly the Lord brought us up from Egypt?' Now the Lord has abandoned us and delivered us into the hands of Midian!" The Lord turned to him and said, "Go in this strength of yours and deliver Israel from the Midianites. I herewith make you my messenger!"

(JUDGES 6:11–14)

"This strength of yours" refers to Gideon's righteous indignation and the fortitude to challenge God.

Gideon couldn't be persuaded to assume the divine mission until he was convinced that he was truly hearing the voice of God through His angel. Gideon challenged the angel to offer miraculous proofs of authenticity, and the angel obliged with three proofs: In the first, Gideon brought a sacrificial offering of meat and bread and placed it upon a rock. The angel touched the offering with the tip of his staff. A fire then sprang up from the rock and consumed the meat and the bread. Thereupon the angel vanished from Gideon's sight. Before the battle against Midian, God himself gratified Gideon's desire for proof that God would be with him in the enterprise. Gideon placed a fleece of wool on the threshing floor and challenged God to have dew fall only on the fleece while the rest of the ground remained dry—which was exactly what Gideon found early the next morning. Still in doubt, Gideon next wanted to see the reverse—"God did so that night: only the fleece was dry, while there was dew all over the ground."

Convinced that God was with him, Gideon accepted his charge, but in dealing with the Midianites, he resorted to nothing miraculous. Brilliant military strategy, both in the drafting of his army and the execution of its battle plans, carried the day for Israelites over Midianites. But Gideon is my favorite Judge for more than just his military prowess.

> Then the men of Israel said to Gideon: "Rule over us—you, your son, and your grandson as well; for you have saved us from the Midianites." But Gideon replied: "I will not rule over you myself, nor shall my son rule over you; the Lord alone shall rule over you."
>
> (JUDGES 8:22, 23)

Gideon shared *his* angel with all of the people.

SOMEWHERE FROM THE area of the Aegean Sea, most probably from the island of Crete, warlike, seafaring peoples came down the Mediterranean and began their incursions into the seacoast areas of Canaan. This happened during the twelfth pre-Christian century, precisely during the period of the Judges. These peoples were the Philistines, and they eventually occupied the major cities of Canaan's coastline, including Gaza, Ashkelon, Ashdod, Ekron, and Gath. They were to prove a thorn in the side of the Israelites for some two hundred years. It was not until King David consolidated his power over all the tribes of Israel that he was able to inflict such serious blows upon the Philistine armies as to greatly reduce their power and effectively remove them as the serious threat they had been to the very survival of Israel in Canaan.

The narrative books of the Hebrew Bible—namely Joshua, Judges, the two Books of Samuel, and the two Books of Kings—represent some of the earliest historical writing of civilized society. The period they cover is from the beginning of the conquest of Canaan—the time of Joshua—to the destruction of the Kingdom of Judah in the year 586 B.C.E.

The biblical narrators make no secret of how they read and interpret their accounts of kings and commoners. They start with the premise that when the people of Israel and their rulers "walk in the way of God" and obey His commandments as transmitted in the Torah received at Sinai, they prosper and hold sway over their enemies. Conversely, their defeat at the hands of enemies is inevitably the result of their "doing that which is bad in the eyes of the Lord" and indulging in the worship of alien gods. This premise is the *leitmotiv* of the whole of the Hebrew Bible. That it did not always fit the facts of Israelite history didn't bother the biblical narrator too much. His purpose was moralistic and didactic. His chronicles, while containing invaluable information and magnificent insights, were tools for the transmission of Judaic monotheism. It is in this light that they should be read and understood.

In the thirteenth chapter of Judges:

The Israelites again did what was offensive to the Lord, and the Lord delivered them into the hands of the Philistines for forty years.

There was a certain man from Zorah, of the stock of Dan, whose name was Manoah. His wife was barren and had borne no children. An angel of the Lord appeared to the woman and said to her, "You are barren and have borne no children; but you shall conceive and bear a son. Now be careful not to drink wine or other intoxicant, or to eat anything unclean. For you are going to conceive and bear a son; let no razor touch his head, for the boy is to be a nazirite to God from the womb on. He shall be the first to deliver Israel from the Philistines."

(JUDGES 13:1-5)

The vision of the angel of the Lord startled and worried Manoah's wife, so she told her husband about it. He prayed to God that the angel might reappear to throw more light on the subject. The angel did return to repeat virtually the same message, this time to both Manoah and his wife. Manoah, not knowing that the messenger (who appeared in human form) was an angel, asked: "What is your name? We should like to honor you when your words come true." The angel responded: "You must not ask for my name; it is unknowable!"

In gratitude, Manoah offered up a sacrifice to God consisting of a kid and a meal offering.

And a marvelous thing happened while Manoah and his wife looked on. As the flames leaped up from the altar toward the sky, the angel of the Lord ascended in the flames of the altar, while Manoah and his wife looked on; and they flung themselves on their faces to the ground . . . Manoah then realized that it had been an angel of the Lord. And Manoah said to his wife, "We shall surely die, for we have seen a divine being." But his wife said to him, "Had the Lord meant to take our lives, He would not have accepted a burnt offering . . . and would not have made such an announcement to us."

The woman bore a son, and she named him Samson. The boy grew up, and the Lord blessed him. The spirit of the Lord first moved him in the encampment of Dan, between Zorah and Eshtaol.

(JUDGES 13:19–25)

Before discussing Samson and his "superman" feats, some consideration should be given to the wife of Manoah, Manoah himself, and the angel of the Lord in this story. To begin with, the name of the key human in the drama, Manoah's wife, is never given. She is clearly more intelligent and of stronger character than her bumbling husband. And it is she who bears both the child and the burden of responsibility for the difficult regimen assigned for him. Those who look for signs of male chauvinism in the Bible will surely find an excellent example here. *Manoah* in Hebrew means "place of refuge." The heroine in our story is therefore best described as the agent of the refuge that her son,

Samson, was to afford his people from the onslaught of the Philistines.

Manoah, on the other hand, is somewhat of a pest. Even though his wife gives him an exact description of her first encounter with the angel, he isn't satisfied: He must see for himself. Then Manoah badgers the angel. Finally he is in anguish when he learns that the encounter was, after all, with a genuine, true-blue angel.

But the angel in the story is of the highest importance. At a time of rampant Philistine idolatry—reflected particularly in Dagon, the deity depicted as half fish and half human—the monotheistic idea had to be driven home sharply. The angel of God directs that Manoah's proffered sacrifice should be to God, not to him. He clearly emphasizes that he is the *agent* of God and that, in and of himself, he has no identity. Having delivered the message, the angel disappears, never again to be seen by Manoah or his wife.

Now as for Samson himself, he has, of course, been a millennial legend. His feats of sheer physical strength include killing a lion by taking hold of its jaws and ripping it in half, destroying a thousand Philistines with the jawbone of an ass, and tying the tails of two hundred foxes to each other. His ultimate undoing by sexy Delilah has become the paradigm for stories of the "La Donna e mobile" genre. The story in Judges ends with the blinded Samson, arms pushed against the pillars of the Temple of Dagon, pleading with God to return his strength—just once—to take revenge on the Philistines, "if only for one of my two eyes." He cries, "Let me die with the Philistines!" as the Temple of Dagon comes crashing down upon both the victim and the victimizers.

*Samson's downfall was made necessary by the very nature of the worldview of the Hebrew Bible.* Samson is the most atypical of Jewish heroes. All brawn and muscle, Samson *is* a Philistine, sharing the Philistines' passion for the exercise of brute force and an orgiastic dedication to the pleasures of the flesh. Samson's victories involve sheer physical power, reflecting the invocation of might as a way of life. For Jews committed to the power of the idea and the ultimate hegemony of truth, Samsonite triumphs are a snare and a delusion.

Like the angel who appeared to Samson's parents to announce his arrival, Samson offered temporary respite from a period of oppression. The *first* to deliver Israel from the Philistines, Samson offered an important lesson about what could and could not save the people. From then on, the Jews would have to look inward for their strength. In the words of the angel of the Lord who speaks to the Hebrew Prince Zerubbabel in the fourth chapter of Zechariah:

> This is the word of the Lord to Zerubbabel: Not my might, nor by power but by My spirit, said the Lord of Hosts.
>
> (ZECHARIAH 4:5)

*The Death of Samson*

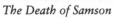

# The Angels of the Book of Daniel

〜〜〜〜〜〜〜〜〜〜〜〜〜〜〜〜〜〜〜〜〜〜〜

The protagonist of the Book of Daniel is as spiritual as Samson was earthy. Depicted as a brilliant young Jew in the service of Babylonian King Nebuchadnezzar, Daniel remained loyal to his monotheistic faith in the very heart of a pagan environment. It is within that environment and through the person of Daniel that a new phenomenon emerges with respect to angels.

None of the angels introduced in the Hebrew Bible up to this point has a name. When pressed by humans to reveal their names, the angels would adamantly refuse: They were agents or messengers of God, with no identity of their own. The Hebrew Bible zealously protected the idea of God's One-ness and was on guard against any implication that His omnipotence might be shared with another being. Moreover, angels are hard to find in the biblical narrative. It takes unusually critical circumstances to bring them into the picture.

Then suddenly in the Book of Daniel, the angelic host— usually described as "The Holy Ones"—is considerably expanded, and two of them are even designated by name: Michael and Gabriel. Both are guardian angels who protect the people of Israel and the *dramatis personae* in the Book of Daniel; namely, Daniel himself and Hananiah, Mishael, and Azariah, also known by their Babylonian names— Shadrach, Meshach, and Abednego.

The Book of Daniel, composed in 164 B.C.E., is the last of the twenty-four books that comprise the Hebrew Bible. It is a visionary work belonging to the genre described as *apocalyptic*. Apocalyptic writing deals with heaven and earth; revelations concerning Creation; the fall of angels and men; the origins of evil; the conflict between light and darkness; hell and heaven; resurrection; last judgment, and the end of days. Most of the books of the Apocrypha belong to this genre and most were composed from about the middle of the second pre-Christian century to about the year 100. The Dead Sea Scrolls, which will be discussed in the following chapter, include considerable apocalyptic writings and therefore abound in angels as well.

Here it is necessary to supply a brief outline of the history of the Jewish people from the beginning of the Babylonian exile to the Maccabean Revolt (586–164 B.C.E.) in order to gain some understanding of the seismic changes wrought in the Jewish psyche that was reflected in the Book of Daniel.

The armies of Nebuchadnezzar, King of Babylon, invaded the Kingdom of Judah in 587 B.C.E., laid siege to its capital, Jerusalem, took the city, and destroyed its Holy Temple. The uninterrupted dynasty of King David was thus brought to an end, and its last monarch, Zedekiah, was blinded and exiled to Babylon along with a large contingent of Jews. They wept "by the waters of Babylon" for their incinerated Temple and their lost glory, and they began to rethink their place in God's scheme of things.

Both the Jews in exile and those who remained in their Holy Land under Babylonian dominion were sustained in their faith by the soaring visions of prophets like the second Isaiah and Ezekiel and Zechariah. Though their styles differed, their message was the same: The people Israel will be comforted by God and He will lead them back to their homeland. Zion will be redeemed in justice and will become a light unto the nations. God will never abandon His people Israel.

The Babylonian empire was overthrown in 539 B.C.E. by Cyrus the Great of Persia, and for about two hundred years after, most of the Jews of the world lived under the aegis of the Persian empire. Generally their treatment was good. They even succeeded in building a second Temple in 517 B.C.E. and in reestablishing the functions of their priesthood and their Torah-guided way of life. Under Ezra and Nehemiah, during the middle of the fifth pre-Christian century, there was a truly epochal religious revival and the beginnings of an all-pervasive, all-embracing legal system in the Holy Land.

In the year 333 B.C.E., Alexander the Great of Macedonia defeated the armies of Persia in the Battle of Issus, so Palestine came under the rule of Alexander and his successors. The Jews there as elsewhere under Hellenistic rule enjoyed religious tolerance for the most part, Alexander having set the example of benevolence. This all came to an abrupt end with the advent of Antiochus IV to the throne of the Seleucid kings, whose dominions included Palestine in 175 B.C.E.

Antiochus was bent on establishing the Greek way of life
—including its religion—throughout his realm, insisting
that all of his subjects submit to the pagan practices of the
state. He ordered the death penalty for the observance of
such basic Jewish rituals as circumcision, the Sabbath, the
dietary laws, and the worship of the One God of Israel. In
effect, he was out to destroy Judaism. He was abetted by
some upperclass Jews who embraced Hellenism, seeking to
cast their destiny with what they perceived to be the wave
of the future.

The ultimate affront to the sensitivities of loyalist Jews—
and they were in the majority—was the placement of a
statue of Zeus (the "Abomination of Desolation" of the
Book of Daniel) in the very heart of the Holy Temple. This
resulted in the Maccabean Revolt, which began in 168
B.C.E., led from its beginning by the priestly family of the
Hasmoneans. Ultimately, Judas Maccabeus succeeded in
ousting the Greek forces from Jerusalem in 164 B.C.E. The
Holy Temple was cleansed and its Judaic rites were rein-
stituted.

It is against the background of the persecutions of Antiochus IV and the chain of events they engendered that the
Book of Daniel was written. The unknown author (or, as
some believe, authors) wrote as if the narrative took place
during the reigns of Babylonian and Persian kings. In this
context, the book was intended to give heart to loyal

Jews struggling to overcome their ordeal under Antiochus.

The Book of Daniel has its own version of the burning bush motif, symbolizing a Jewry surviving despite the flames of Antiochus's fury. In the third chapter of Daniel, King Nebuchadnezzar erected a golden idol on the Plain of Dura in Babylon and ordered all of his people to prostrate themselves before it and worship it or face the penalty of death. Three young Jews—Shadrach, Meshach, and Abednego—refused to do the king's bidding. As punishment, Nebuchadnezzar ordered the three rebellious Jews to be bound in fetters and cast into the raging flames of a furnace. When the king looked into the furnace, he was astounded by what he saw: Four men completely unharmed, walking about freely in the fire. The fourth man was an angel.

> Nebuchadnezzar then went near the opening of the white-hot furnace and said: "Shadrach, Meshach and Abednego, servants of the Most High God, come out here." Thereupon Shadrach, Meshach and Abednego came out of the fire . . . the hair of their head was not singed, and their clothes were not affected; not even a smell of fire came from them.
>
> Nebuchadnezzar said, "Blessed be the God of Shadrach, Meshach and Abednego, because he sent his angel and rescued his servants who trusted in him; disregarding the King's orders, they yielded up their bodies rather than serve or worship any God but their own . . . there is no other god who can effect such a rescue." (DANIEL 3:26–29)

The reference to the Jewish condition under Antiochus IV is clear, as is the description of Jews fiercely loyal to their monotheistic tradition. The author(s) of the Book of Daniel had no doubt that the guardian angel of the Jewish people would save them from the savagery of Antiochus and that Judaism and its adherents would emerge unscathed from the fires of the enemy.

But Daniel, the angelic companion of Shadrach, Meshach, and Abednego, was not satisfied with a miraculous escape from the furnace. Deeply troubled about the future of his people, he worried about their ability to triumph over the kingdoms of paganism that successively ruled over them. By day, Daniel would pray to God for answers, and by night, his preoccupations were manifested in dreams that the Archangels Gabriel and Michael would interpret for him. Again, they were the only angels designated by name in the Hebrew Bible, most likely because the Jewish people desperately needed a more concrete vision of God's intervention on their behalf during such trying times. The names also brought them closer to the God who seemed to have distanced Himself from His people as their Holy Temple was destroyed and a succession of enemies—Babylonians, Persians, Medes, and Greeks—took turns undermining the foundations of Judaic survival.

Michael and Gabriel were more than simply interpreters of Daniel's vision. They also depicted events of the future in a way designed to brighten the hearts of the Jewish people during the dark Maccabean era. The angelic forecast included the pronouncement that "the kingship and dominion and the grandeur of all the kingdoms under the heavens will be given to the people of the holy ones of the Most High. Their royal rule will last forever, and all the dominions will serve and obey it."

For the first time in the Hebrew Bible, angels were forecasting a distant future. It is no accident that this happened toward the very end of the biblical period, about the year 170 B.C.E. The anguish of the Jewish people under the rule of the Syrian-Greeks, the threat to the very survival of their religion, and the diminishing role of the Promised Land in their lives led the Jews into a state of despair. While they didn't lose their faith in the God of Israel, they did begin to doubt the imminence of their redemption. The reassurances of the Archangels Michael and Gabriel as prophets possibly rescued the national morale.

Michael and Gabriel appear again and again in the role of Israel's guardian angels. For after the era in which the Book of Daniel was written, and despite a century of central Jewish government within the borders of an expanded Jewish state, there was always a threat to Israel's national independence. For the next two millennia, their history would be largely diaspora history. A pessimistic vision once again permeated the writing of apocalyptic texts. Imperial Rome began to choke the life out of the rebellious spirit of fiercely nationalist Judeans, as the Jewish community of Palestine fragmented. When it was most needed, a united front was conspicuously absent. Sects multiplied, and one of these sects set up its headquarters in the Judean desert by the Dead Sea not far from the city of Jericho at whose walls Joshua had sounded the trumpets heralding the beginning of Jewish statehood.

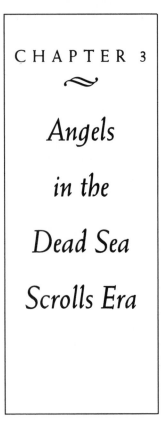

CHAPTER 3

*Angels*

*in the*

*Dead Sea*

*Scrolls Era*

## The Scroll People

In 1947 an Arab shepherd boy accidentally stumbled upon what was to prove to be the most sensational archaeological find of this century. In one of the caves of

Qumran at the northern end of the Dead Sea, he found several ancient scrolls that had been placed in jars to afford some protection from the elements.

A year later, the newly formed state of Israel managed to procure the seven scrolls. A frenzy of exploration followed during which scores of caves in the Qumran area were searched, yielding hundreds of fragments of ancient writing that ultimately came under the control of the government of Jordan and were housed mainly in the Rockefeller Museum in East Jerusalem. An international team of specialists was entrusted with the task of studying and publishing the vast materials, though precious little has been published to date.

By 1991, the outcry against what many scholars perceived as a stonewalling operation reached the front pages of newspapers around the world and impassioned charges and countercharges polluted the air of scholarship. The situation reached a climax when the Huntington Library in Pasadena, California, disclosed that it had a complete set of photographs of all unpublished Dead Sea Scroll material and would make it available to any qualified scholar for study and commentary.

What we know so far is based on the publication of the Israeli-owned Scrolls. Israeli scholars edited and annotated editions of the Scrolls titled *The Manual of Discipline, The War of the Sons of Light Against the Sons of Darkness, The Thanksgiving Hymns, A Genesis Apocryphon*, and *The Habakkuk Commentary*.

Hundreds of books and articles have been published on the Scrolls, and hundreds more are in the offing. Despite contradictory opinions about the time, the identity, the history, and the beliefs of the people who wrote these Scrolls, that they were Palestinian Jews has never been contested. Neither has the residence of those people in the Qumran area been in doubt. The ruins of the buildings in which they lived and worked have been excavated, and it is estimated that the space was home to some two hundred of them.

Most likely, the Scroll people belonged to the Jewish sect known as the Essenes, who are treated somewhat briefly in the writings of Josephus, Pliny the Elder, and Philo. The Essenes were ascetics who gathered into communal groups, eschewed the quest of luxury, worked hard to eke out their livelihood, believed that they were the elect, or the chosen of Israel—the only ones who adhered to the true covenant of the Lord with His people Israel. They believed that by so doing they would hasten the advent of messianic times and bring each of them closer to the divine.

Imposing the strictest forms of discipline upon themselves, they also prepared for the imminent apocalyptic battle between the Sons of Light (themselves) and the Sons of Darkness (those who had strayed from the covenant and were led by the forces of Belial, which included all the enemies of the Jewish people).

The Scrolls sect believed that the world of their day was in control of Belial and his evil forces. But they also believed that the showdown battle against Belial was near.

The author of *The War of the Sons of Light Against the Sons of Darkness* was confident of the approaching victory of the Sons of Light because he lived at "a time of mighty trouble for the people to be redeemed by God." He founded his belief on the following passage from Daniel:

> At that time Michael, the great prince, the protector of your people, will arise. It will be a time of distress, such as never occurred since nations came into being until that time. But at that time your people will be rescued, every one of them who is found written in the book.
>
> (DANIEL 12:1)

The concept of the Sons of Light in mortal combat with the Sons of Darkness represented something new within Judaism and was in some way a manifestation of the dualistic doctrine propounded by Zoroaster about the year 600 B.C.E. Zoroaster had taught that there were two spirits in the world: One, the progenitor and propagator of evil, lived in darkness, and the other, devoted to goodness, dwelled in light. The goal of humans was to escape the snares of the evil spirit, Ahriman, and to embrace the spirit of light, Ahura-Mazda. These spirits, meanwhile, were engaged in constant war for the soul of man. Zoroaster believed that in the end good would prevail over evil and light would banish darkness in this epic struggle.

Some Dead Sea Scroll scholars believe that the teaching of Zoroaster significantly influenced the Scroll people's concept of an apocalyptic war of the "Sons of Light against the Sons of Darkness." The following passage from one of the very important Dead Sea Scrolls, *The Manual of Discipline*, makes this clear:

Now, this God created man to rule the world, and appointed for him two spirits after whose direction he was to walk until the final Inquisition. They are the spirits of truth and of perversity.

The origin of truth lies in the Fountain of Light, and that of perversity in the Wellspring of Darkness. All who practice righteousness are under the domination of the Prince of Lights, and walk in ways of light; whereas all who practice perversity are under the domination of the Angel of Darkness and walk in ways of darkness. Through the Angel of Darkness, however, even those who practice righteousness are made liable to error. All their sin and their iniquities, all their guilt and their deeds of transgression are the result of his domination; and this, by God's inscrutable design, will continue until the time appointed by Him. Moreover, all men's afflictions and all their moments of tribulation are due to this being's malevolent sway. All of the spirits that attend upon him are bent on causing the sons of light to stumble. Howbeit, the God of Israel and the Angel of His truth are always there to help the sons of light. It is God that created these spirits of light and darkness and made them the basis of every act, the [instigators] of every deed and the directors of every thought. The one He loves to all eternity, and is ever pleased with its deeds; but any asso-

ciation with the other He abhors, and He hates all its ways
to the end of time.[1]

(GASTER: *THE DEAD SEA SCRIPTURES* P. 43, 44)

The Scroll people gave emphasis to one of the fundamental themes of the Hebrew Bible; namely, that the potential
for both good and evil is inherent in all human beings ever
since Adam and Eve ate the forbidden fruit. The expulsion
of Adam and Eve from the Garden of Eden was the result of
the triumph of the evil inclination, as symbolized by the
Serpent, over the good impulse, the word of God. Moses,
the great lawgiver himself, puts the concept clearly before
his people Israel in one of his farewell orations in Deuteronomy:

> "See, I set before you this day life and prosperity, death and
> adversity. . . . Therefore choose life!"
>
> (DEUTERONOMY 30:15)

In the teachings of Moses and the prophets up to the time
of the destruction of the First Commonwealth and its Holy
Temple in 586 B.C.E., good and evil are abstract concepts.
But shortly after that, as a result of the Jews' close contact
with Persian (Iranian) culture and the religion of Zoroaster, which prevailed during the Persian era of Jewish
history (540–330 B.C.E.), "good" and "evil" were gradually

personified. Thus, for example, in the Book of Zechariah, a prophet who lived toward the end of the sixth pre-Christian century, there was a confrontation between the angel of the Lord and Satan:

> He showed me Joshua the high priest standing before the angel of the Lord, and Satan standing at his right hand as his adversary.
>
> (ZECHARIAH 3:1)

This passage becomes most illuminating if we examine the context in which Joshua, the High Priest, and Zerubbabel, the descendant of the House of David, appeared on the scene. The Persian King Cyrus had authorized the Jews who wished to do so to return from Babylonia to Jerusalem and to rebuild their Holy Temple. Under the leadership of Zerubbabel several thousand Jews did indeed return, but they were stunned by the devastation they found and depressed by the poverty of the Jews who had remained in Jerusalem and its vicinity. The Babylonian Jews, who had left relative comfort behind because of their religious zeal and the hope they could find a semblance of their past glories in the ancestral home, started thinking that rebuilding the Temple was an impossible task—especially if it were to bear any resemblance to the magnificent Temple built by Solomon about 940 B.C.E., four hundred years before.

The two leaders, Zerubbabel and Joshua, the prince and the priest, began to bicker, and two of the prophets, Haggai

THE ARK OF THE COVENANT ... ND A CLOUD ABOVE BE
SHEWING Y BARRS ON Y SIDE ... WEEN Y CHERUBIMS WHICH
ACCORDING TO L KINGS VIII. 8 ... EMS TO SHINE AND, AS TO BE
THE CHERUBIMS ABOVE ON ... WERE EMBRACED BY
THE COVERING, EACH WITH ... INGS OF Y CHERUBIMS
TWO WINGS WITHOUT HANDS ... according to Schacovte & others

*The Temple*
*of Solomon*

and Zechariah, were in the middle. Both prophets argued strongly for beginning the work of Temple construction. Haggai prophesied that the glory of the second house of God would exceed even that of the first and that physical dimensions had nothing to do with spiritual attainment. Zechariah felt that the malaise afflicting the people and their leaders was the work of a Satan born out of the people's doubts about themselves, their God, and their destiny. Zechariah called upon his people to summon forth their better angel, the angel of hope and optimism. As inspiration, he relayed this vision of the angel of the Lord addressing Satan:

> "The Lord rebuke you, O Satan! May the Lord who has chosen Jerusalem rebuke you! Is this not a brand plucked from the fire?"
>
> (ZECHARIAH 3:2)

Satan is drawn to the fires of disaster as swine are drawn to refuse. He can only be fended off by the saving angel of the Lord who opposes the vision of life to that of death, who urges the storm-swept sailor to sail on, who arms the mason with the trowel and bids him "build!"

≈ ≈ ≈

# Pharisees, Sadducees, and Essenes

The Jews in their Holy Land were "a brand plucked from the fire" when the Scroll people first appeared. Many scholars of the Dead Sea sect trace their emergence to the Hasideans, the fiercely loyal Jews of the Maccabean Revolt. Again, as during the Persian era, the Temple of the Lord was at the center of events. It had to be wrested from the defiling hands of the Hellenistic enemy. The Maccabean rulers, successors of Judah Maccabee, had reestablished Jewish sovereignty in the homeland for almost a hundred years. But in 63 B.C.E. the Roman General Pompey invaded Jerusalem, and the land of the Jews—Judaea, as the Romans called it—became another puppet state in a vast empire.

Again and again the national and religious passion of the Jews bred riots and outbreaks against the occupying power. Again "unmerciful disaster followed fast and followed faster,"[2] and factionalism was rife amongst the Jews in Israel: There were incurable rebels who dared dream that David could once again slay Goliath with a slingshot. There were confirmed pacifists who saw no hope for the Jews except in passive accommodation with the Romans and continued self-consecration to God and Torah. And there was the Sadducee party, which claimed that the best policy to follow was to do as the Romans did, even in their native city of Jerusalem. These political factions had sharp religious differences as well. The Sadducee party, made up of well-to-do and influential Temple priests, harked back to the old days when the priest was teacher of the law as well as officiant of the Temple cult. But beginning with the days of Ezra (around 450 B.C.E.), a tradition of scholarship that was independent of priestly sway emerged. In the early days these scholars were called scribes (*Soferim*) and gradually they became the party of the Pharisees, earning the respect of most of their coreligionists because of both their wide learning and their nobility of character. Ultimately, the Pharisees became the architects of the Mishnah, the first code of Jewish law since the legislation in the Pentateuch.

Then there were the Essenes, whom most scholars identify as the Scroll people. This group felt that *they* were the saving remnant, the "brand plucked from the fire." They turned their backs on the establishment and set out to live their lives in their own idiosyncratic ways. Though their numbers were small, their dedication to what they perceived to be the rightness of their cause was all-consuming. Apparently they had at one time had a charismatic leader whom they called "The Teacher of Righteousness." What became of him is unclear, though some scholars read into a vague passage in the Scroll writings that he was murdered, and perhaps became the model for the crucified Jesus. What is clear, however, is that the Teacher of Righteousness was opposed by an enemy designated as the Wicked

Priest, also referred to as Belial ("Son of Evil"). The dominant Scrolls' scenario is a battle to the finish between these two forces, the Sons of Light and the Sons of Darkness.

The Scroll people were certain that they would ultimately prevail over the forces of darkness that dominated the world at the time. There would be an armageddon in which the "brand plucked from the fire" would kindle a conflagration that would incinerate darkness and evil.

The Sons of Light had many angels in their armies. And the Sons of Darkness had angels of destruction.

THE HEBREW BIBLE consistently focused on the destiny of the people Israel rather than that of the individual Jew. Prosperity and well-being were measured by a national yardstick. If all went well with the nation, God was keeping His side of the covenant and advancing the good of the people. That, of course, was dependent upon the people's adhering to their side of the covenant—walking in the ways of God and scrupulously adhering to His Torah. When the Jewish people failed to do so they were punished as God allowed their enemies to gain the upper hand.

Within the scheme of this historiographic theory (which did not always accommodate the facts), the lot of the individual was largely overlooked. Salvation was for the people as a whole, not for its individual members. During most of the biblical period the symbol of salvation for the Children of Israel was the Exodus from Egypt and the ultimately successful return to the land of their fathers.

Continuous battering and suffering at the hands of one enemy after another led the individual to ponder the problem of his own suffering and to become obsessed with his personal salvation. Finally, for the first time, the idea of resurrection was articulated in the Book of Daniel—chronologically, the last of the books of the Hebrew Bible. The questioning of God's justice probably began with the Babylonian exile. The biblical books written after that disaster include Ecclesiastes and Job, both of which attempted to deal with the problem in different ways. Job's powerful affirmation—"I know that my redeemer exists"—was made in the face of hellish personal disasters.

As the process of individuation of suffering unfolded, so did the emphasis on personal angels. For it became clear to those who pondered the problem of national suffering and humiliation that salvation for the *people* Israel was not at hand. It would have to await some far-off messianic day. But in the meantime it was necessary to sustain the spirit of individual Jews lest there be no soldiers to fight the decisive battle of light and good against darkness and evil. In the Dead Sea Scrolls there was a clear tendency to implant angels of light into the souls of good individuals so that they might be fortified for the ultimate and inevitable showdown with angels of darkness who dominated the souls of evil folk. But even good people were sometimes tested by angels of darkness, just as evil people have angels of light.

The Scroll titled *The Manual of Discipline*, which may be described as the constitution and by-laws of the sect, says:

This is the way those spirits operate in the world. The enlightenment of man's heart, the making straight before him all the ways of righteousness and truth, the implanting in his heart of fear for the judgments of God, of a spirit of humility, of patience, of abundant compassion . . . of a spirit of knowledge informing every plan of action . . . of a hallowed mind in a controlled nature, of abounding love for all who follow the truth, of a self-respecting purity which abhors all the taint of filth . . . these are the things that come to men in this world through communion with the spirit of truth. And the guerdon (reward) of all that walk in its ways is health and abundant well being, with long life and fruition of seed along with eternal blessings and everlasting joy in the life everlasting, and a crown of glory and a robe of honor amid light perpetual.

But to the spirit of perversity (the Angel of Darkness) belong greed, remissness in rightdoing, wickedness and falsehood, pride and presumption, deception and guile, cruelty and abundant insolence, shortness of temper and profusion of folly, arrogant passion, abominable acts in a spirit of lewdness, filthy ways to the thralldom of unchastity, a blasphemous tongue, blindness of eyes, dullness of ears, stiffness of neck and hardness of heart, to the end that a man walks entirely in ways of darkness and of evil cunning. The guerdon of all who walk in such ways is multitude of afflictions at the hands of all the angels of destruction, everlasting perdition through the angry wrath of an avenging God, eternal horror and perpetual reproach, the disgrace of final annihilation in the Fire . . . ending in extinction without remnant or survival.

It is to these things that all men are born, and it is to these that all the host of them are heirs throughout their generations. It is in these ways that men must walk and it is in these two divisions, according as a man inherits something of each, that all human acts are decided throughout all the ages of eternity. For God has appointed these two things to obtain in equal measure until the final age . . . He will determine the fate of every living being in accordance with which of the (two spirits) he has chosen to follow.[3]

In sum, within every human are two angels: the Angel of Light and the Angel of Darkness. The one tends to promote all that is good; the other, all that is evil. Every human deed strengthens the hand of one angel or the other. So personal salvation is something that can be won or lost by the works of the individual. In this belief, the Scroll people were fully in accord with the doctrine of normative Judaism.

While the Scrolls repeatedly stress the will of God in choosing those destined to be among the blessed—the Sons of Light—and those destined to be counted among the cursed Sons of Darkness, it seems clear that the Scroll people did not regard these choices as arbitrary. God's knowledge of everything that was, is, and is to be would determine His choices. But the individual chooses his actions. That, too, is a fundamental Judaic doctrine that is taught in so many biblical tales—the Adam and Eve narrative, the

Cain and Abel tragedy, Noah's defiance of the corruption of his generation, and Joseph's resistance to the sexual advances of Potiphar's wife—to mention only a few of the confrontations between good and evil, all in the very first book of the Hebrew Bible. The prophets of Israel, from Amos (eighth century B.C.E.) through Malachi (fourth century B.C.E.), endlessly and tirelessly stressed the role of human choice as decisive in the destinies of both individuals and nations.

For the Scroll people, the yearning for personal salvation was acute—to be in the company of the angels was the ultimate in bliss. The life of the Scroll people was defined by an incessant longing for proximity to God and His blessed company of angels.

To the Scroll people the doomed doers of evil were those who followed Belial, the Angel of Darkness and destruction. Belial is mentioned no less than thirty-three times in portions of the Dead Sea Scrolls published so far. The Scroll people saw their own time as the era of Belial's dominion. But Belial figures prominently in the books of the Apocrypha and Pseudepigrapha as well, most notably in the Book of Jubilees and the Testament of the Tribes.

≈ ≈ ≈

# Apocrypha and Pseudepigrapha

～～～～～～～～～～～～～～～～～～～～～～～～

The books of the Apocrypha and Pseudepigrapha were written during the intertestamentary period; that is, from about the beginning of the second century B.C.E. to the end of the second century C.E., *precisely the time period of the Scroll people. Apocryphon* in Greek means "hidden," and in the literary area it described writing that contained "secret" teaching that was to be reserved for the specially selected or the initiate. Ultimately, the term *Apocrypha* (the plural form) was applied to books of a religious nature that were *not* included in the Hebrew Bible. Most of the books of the Apocrypha were written by Jews, in either Hebrew or Aramaic.

The Pseudepigrapha consist of books attributed by the author to great figures of past centuries, most of whom are mentioned in the Hebrew Bible. These include, among others, Enoch, Abraham, Moses, Solomon, Isaiah, and Ezra. There is nothing "pseudo" about these writings except their attribution to better or lesser known biblical personalities—a technique for getting the reader's attention that was quite common then. The exclusion of both Apocrypha and Pseudepigrapha from the Hebrew Bible resulted in their gradual disappearance from the Jewish scene. It is thanks to their translation into Greek and the preservation of many of them as an integral part of the Bible of the Catholic church that these books have survived.

We already know that the Jewish sacred Scriptures, the *Kittevei haKodesh*, were officially edited, adopted, and "canonized" by the great rabbinic authorities toward the middle of the second century. In the Talmud, some of the debates and controversies associated with this process are recorded.

The books of the Apocrypha and Pseudepigrapha, although they were in some ways related to biblical style and subject matter and were thoroughly religious in nature, were viewed by the Rabbis as dangerous to the faith for many reasons. Their apocalyptic hysteria, for one, was deemed detrimental to the Jewish state of mind during the terribly troubled years following the destruction of the Holy Temple in the year 70. The physical attributes of God they describe were disrespectful of the idea of God's incorporeality, which had been for so many centuries a central pillar of the Jewish faith. But most disturbing of all to the Rabbis was the "population explosion" of angels to the point that they nearly overwhelmed the Creator Himself. A thousand-year angelic role as creatures and messengers of the Deity was being subverted by an Apocryphal, apocalyptic lore that, to the Rabbis, threatened to inundate Judaism with a new form of idolatry.

Consider the variety of angelic names and functions from just one modest list in the book of 3 Enoch:

> Gabriel, the angel of fire;
> Baradiel, the angel of hail;

Ruhiel, who is in charge of wind;
Baraquiel, who is in charge of lightning;
Za'amiel, who is in charge of whirlwind;
Ziquiel, who is in charge of comets;
Zi'iel, who is in charge of tremors;
Za'apiel, who is in charge of hurricane;
Ra'amiel, who is in charge of thunder;
Ra'asiel, who is in charge of earthquakes;
Shalgiel, who is in charge of snow;
Matariel, who is in charge of rain;
Shimshiel, who is in charge of day;
Lailiel, who is in charge of night;
Galgalliel, who is in charge of the orb of the sun;
Opanniel, who is in charge of the disk of the moon;
Kokabriel, who is in charge of the stars;
Rahatiel, who is in charge of the constellations.[4]

The names of these angels are manufactured from the nature of their assignments, and there is an almost atavistic regression to a pagan pantheon in which a god corresponds to nearly every natural phenomenon. The Greek and Roman pantheons, among others, assigned gods and goddesses for every major force in nature. The Rabbis felt that the Apocrypha and Pseudepigrapha, with their profusion of angelic names and functions comparable to Greek and Roman gods and goddesses, posed a threat to Judaic monotheism. So the Rabbis suppressed and condemned all of the writing in this genre.

For all of the hundreds of angels named in the Apocrypha and Pseudepigrapha, an extraordinary number remain incognito, as witnessed by Enoch, among others. Enoch, one of the enigmas in the story of Genesis, "walked with God; then he was no more, for God took him" (Genesis 6:24). This unique and mysterious reference to Enoch's death, plus the fact that Enoch died at a mere 365 — the shortest life span of his genealogy (his son Methuselah lived to be 969) — supplied an Enoch mythology of no less than three versions in the Pseudepigrapha. In all the versions Enoch is transported live to the heavens. In Enoch I, a fragment of which was also found among the Dead Sea Scrolls, he reports:

> I saw a hundred thousand times a hundred thousand, ten million times ten million, an innumerable and uncountable (multitude) who stand before the glory of the Lord of the Spirits.

The same passage, however, rapidly leaves the "innumerable" to introduce only four angels by name:

> I saw them standing — on the four wings of the Lord of the Spirits — and saw four other faces among those who do not slumber, and I came to know their names, which the angel who came with me revealed to me . . . I heard the voices of those four faces while they were saying praises before the Lord of Glory . . . And after that, I asked the angel of peace who was going with me and showed me everything that was hidden: "Who are these four faces which I have seen?" . . . And he said, to me, "The first one is the merciful and for-

bearing Michael; the second one, who is set over all disease and every wound of the children of the people, is Raphael; the third, who is set over all exercise of strength is Gabriel; and the fourth, who is set over all actions of repentance unto the hope of those who would inherit eternal life, is Phanuel (in other versions, Uriel) by name."[5]

This exclusive quartet are closest to the throne of God, the inner circle of the divine presence (in Hebrew, *Malak-hei Ha-pnim*). The first book of Enoch adds three more to the angelic elite known as archangels: Sariel, whose duties are undefined; Jeremiel, who has charge of souls in the underworld; and Raguel, one of the holy angels, who take vengeance for the world and for the luminaries. (I have yet to find a satisfactory explanation for this last job description from Pseudepigrapha scholars.)

## Metatron

The angel Metatron plays a very important role in the Pseudepigrapha, the Talmud, and, especially, the *Zohar*, masterwork of the Kabbala. In the *Hebrew Book of Enoch* Enoch becomes Metatron as soon as he, Enoch, is translated live into heaven (Genesis 5:21–24). In that work, Enoch describes the transformation of his earthly body into a fiery flame.

Shortly after Enoch-Metatron's arrival in heaven he is assigned one of the central roles within the gathering of angels. His tasks are varied: he ministers to the Throne of Glory where God Himself is ensconced; he is the High Priest of the heavenly Temple; he is in charge of the guardian angels assigned to the metaphorical "seventy peoples of the world"; he is the minister of wisdom who also holds the keys to the mysteries of all matters divine.

The *Zohar* describes the actual mechanism behind mortal Enoch's transformation into the heavenly Metatron. When Adam sinned in the Garden of Eden he lost the divine spark which God had set into his body at its creation. That spark entered into Enoch, enabling him to fulfill the spiritual perfection Adam had failed to attain. Since perfection cannot reside with fallible mortals, Enoch had to be transported to heaven to become the angel Metatron.

The flames that perpetually emerge from Metatron engender armies of angels, for his name is the numerical equivalent of *Shaddai*, one of the several descriptions of God Himself. (Mystical numerology, known as *Gematria*, assigns a numerical value to each letter of the Hebrew alphabet. The Hebrew letters of both Metatron and Shaddai add up to 314.) This is already implied in the Talmud which affirms that Metatron's name is like unto that of his Master. Hence the *Zohar* speaks of Metatron as "The shining light of the *Shekhina*," or the divine presence.

The *Zohar* relates that Metatron was created before anything earthly since he was to represent a kind of microcos-

mic spiritual perfection, utterly free from baseness and impurities.

Ironically, in a later Zoharic work, the *Tikkunei Zohar*,
Metatron is identified as the biblical "tree of knowledge of
good and bad." There the idea is developed that in Metatron are combined both human and angelic perfection.
This unique situation renders Metatron supremely qualified to mediate between the human and the divine. But in
order to do so, Metatron requires the help of the righteous
on earth whose good deeds generate the spiritual energy he
needs to maintain his vitality. Without this energy, Metatron is weakened, as are humanity's prospects of redemption through union with the divine.

In its depiction of Metatron as the Tree of Knowledge of
Good and Bad, the *Zohar* presents an angel as metaphor
for human struggle. The microcosmic vehicle for human
salvation is the resolution of the conflict between good and
evil. The battle must be waged within each of us in order to
eradicate evil—the ultimate purpose for the gathering of
the angels within each of us.

≈ ≈ ≈

# THE ANGELIC INNER CIRCLE

## Michael

~ ~ ~ ~ ~ ~ ~ ~ ~ ~ ~ ~ ~ ~ ~ ~ ~ ~ ~ ~ ~ ~ ~ ~ ~

"Merciful-and-forbearing" Michael emerges from age-old Jewish literature as the commander-in-chief of the entire angelic host and as the angel specifically assigned to be the guardian of Israel. In 3 Baruch, a book in the Pseudepigrapha, Michael is the holder of the keys to the heavenly kingdom. There, as in many other places in the Pseudepigrapha, he is the angel who accepts the prayers and offerings of man and transmits them to God—a task contrary to a long-cherished Jewish belief that there are no intermediaries between man's prayers and God. Such a departure from a major article of Judaic faith was the result of widespread sentiment that God had temporarily withdrawn from His people on account of their sinfulness at this particular time in history, and that pending His return (which the faithful did not doubt for a moment), angels such as Michael served as the intermediate address for the people's prayers. Still, Michael himself did not respond to prayers—he simply delivered them to God and returned with a verdict of acceptance or rejection depending on the truthfulness and the quality of the prayers and of the people who did the offering.

"Merciful-and-forbearing" Michael would not act in

that role on judgment day. When the angels of corruption and destruction were finally brought to justice, Michael joined Raphael, Gabriel, and Phanuel (Uriel) as the executors of the divine will. The scene is described in 1 Enoch:

> Then I looked and turned to another face of the earth and saw there a valley, deep and burning with fire. And they were bringing kings and potentates and were throwing them into this deep valley. And my eyes saw there their chains while they were making them into iron fetters of immense weight. And I asked the angel of peace who was going with me, saying, "For whom are these imprisonment chains being prepared?" And he said unto me, "These are being prepared for the armies of Azazel, in order that they may take them and cast them into the abyss of complete condemnation, and as the Lord of the Spirits has commanded it, they shall cover their jaws with rocky stones. Then Michael, Raphael, Gabriel and Phanuel themselves shall seize them on that great day of judgment and cast them into the furnace that is burning that day, so that the Lord of the Spirits may take vengeance on them on account of their oppressive deeds which they performed as messengers of Satan, leading astray those who dwell upon the earth.[6]

This seminal passage in the thinking of both the Scroll people and the Pseudepigraphic writers provides sweeping answers to abiding theological questions about God and humanity, evil and corruption, faith and fate, despair and hope.

*How account for evil in a world created by a God who is all good?* Rebellious angels leave the divine presence and descend to earth to debase man, thereby engendering evil. *How can evil be overcome?* By harnessing the angelic forces for good that are always there for those who choose them. *What can man himself do to accelerate the eradication of evil?* He can begin to control evil by subduing his own corrupt inclinations and mastering his own satanic potential.

Through all this miasma of apocalyptic imagery the basic Judaic theodicy still shines: There are both Michaels and Azazels within us; Princes of Light and Princes of Darkness. And it is up to us to choose. As Moses said at the very outset of Israel's career as the people of God, "Behold I place before you life and good, as well as death and evil; therefore choose life!"

The Archangel Michael is also a celestial historiographer. In 1 Enoch he has these remarkable words to say:

> "For indeed human beings were not created but to be like angels, permanently to maintain pure and righteous lives. Death, which destroys everything, would have not touched them, had it not been through their knowledge by which they shall perish. *Death is now eating us by means of this power*" (italics added).

When Adam and Eve ate of the forbidden fruit—that of the Tree of Knowledge of Good and Bad—they acquired the capacity to create and destroy with their new knowledge. Advances in science and technology have exponentially increased the human means of destruction. The splitting of the atom, for example, has unleashed power of unimagined destructiveness. And as prophesized in 1 Enoch, "Death is now eating us by means of this power."

I must share an encounter I had in Nagasaki in 1952 with a survivor of the atomic bomb. I was on my way back to the States after having completed a tour of duty as a chaplain in Korea. I visited the Nagasaki museum, which depicts graphically some of what was wrought there on August 9, 1945, and found myself sobbing like an infant. A gentle touch on my arm turned my attention to a singular woman: She had one eye, one foot, one ear—and two crutches. She spoke to me in English: "Please, please do not weep for the dead and the torn. Weep instead for the living and the well. We have learned the ways of death. But we have not yet learned the way to life."

How well we know Azazel. How little we know Michael.

## Tobit and Raphael

~~~~~~~~~~~~~~~~~~~~~~~~~~~~~~~~~~~~~~~~~~~~~

Do we know the Archangel Raphael at all? He did not get the press that Michael or Gabriel enjoyed. And yet as the healing angel, it is Raphael who may be the closest to us. His Hebrew name means "Heal me, O God!"

Once upon a time, long, long ago, in the city of Nineveh, there lived a very good Jew named Tobit, according to the book of the Apocrypha that bears his name. Along with thousands of his people he had been forced into exile from his native land of Israel by Shalmaneser, the Assyrian King who conquered the Holy Land. Tobit was a man who lived a life of charity toward both the living and the dead. He gave food to the hungry, he clothed the naked, he housed the homeless, he comforted the bereaved, and above all, he buried the dead, even at the risk of his own life—as it was then a capital offense to inter the dead bodies of the King's enemies.

For this last of Tobit's many kindnesses he had had to run for his life and had suffered the confiscation of all his property. His wife, Hannah, had to eke out their livelihood when, through an eerie mishap, Tobit went blind. On the brink of despair, Tobit prayed fervently to God that his life might be ended and thus bring an end to his suffering. Only his loyalty to Hannah and love for their one child, Tobias, stayed his hand from suicide.

Another prayer reached heaven simultaneously from Sarah, daughter of Tobit's brother, who lived in the city Ecbatana in Media. Sarah also had her troubles: She buried seven husbands because the evil demon Asmodeus killed them (for reasons unspecified) on their wedding nights.

"You know, Lord (Sarah prayed) that I am innocent of any sin with man; I have never defiled my name, or the name of my father, in the land of my captivity. I am my father's only child . . . I have already lost seven husbands; why must I live any longer?"

And the prayer of both of them was heard in the presence of the glory of the great Raphael, and he was sent to cure them both; for Tobit, to remove the white films (cataracts), and to give Sarah, the daughter of Raguel, to Tobit's son Tobias, as his wife, and to bind Asmodeus, the wicked demon, because Tobias was entitled to possess her.[7]

Tobias, as the story unfolds, was sent by Tobit on a journey that ultimately brought him to Sarah's home in Media. The angel Raphael in human disguise became the traveling companion of Tobias, with his father's blessing:

"Go with this man, and God who lives in heaven will prosper your journey, and let his angel go with you."[8]

Raphael, of course, performed his assignment to perfection. Using his angelic expertise, he exorcised the demon Asmodeus from the psyche of Sarah and bestowed his protective presence upon her eighth husband. And he restored Tobit's vision.

Toward the end, Raphael revealed his identity:

"I will not conceal anything from you; as I said, it is wise to keep a King's secret, but the works of God should be gloriously revealed. So now when you and your daughter-in-law Sarah prayed, I brought the remembrance of your prayer before the Holy One. And when you buried the dead, I was still with you . . . your good deed did not escape me, but I was with you. So God sent me to cure you and your daughter-in-law Sarah. For I am Raphael, one of the seven holy angels, who offer up the prayers of God's people and go into the presence of the glory of the Holy One."[9]

It is an imperfect assumption that prayer is a plea to God on our own behalf or even on behalf of others. While that's certainly a legitimate part of praying, there is a more profound dimension of prayer: addressing the noble and the true and the beautiful within us as we contemplate the ultimate in goodness and unselfishness that we profess to see in God. Prayers are answered when we fulfill each other's needs. Tobit's angel saw his need as he intercepted Tobit's prayer. Sarah's angel saw her needs as soon as her lamentation reached him. The angel in both cases was the healing Raphael, who clearly perceived that the cure consisted in bringing Tobit and Sarah together through the medium of Tobias, who was son to one and husband to the other. "He prayeth best who loveth best" because he is in possession of the best medicine for most ailments: love.

≈ ≈ ≈

# Gabriel

~~~~~~~~~~~~~~~~~~~~~~~~~~~~~~~~~~~~~~~~~~

So we have the quality of mercy in the Archangel Michael and love in the Archangel Raphael. What quality is embodied in the Archangel Gabriel? Christians might say a trumpeter par excellence. Jewish lore depicts him as a master of courage.

When Enoch, a human, was transported to heaven, he was overwhelmed with fear and awed by the dazzling spectacle surrounding him. Although he was accompanied on his celestial journey by an angel of peace, he became increasingly agitated as he got closer to the throne of God Himself. Could a mortal even think of an encounter with the Creator? Would not the very thought be blasphemous? Could he absorb the sheer shock of it and still remain a living human being, albeit a stranger in paradise?

It was Gabriel who gave Enoch the courage for this encounter: "Be brave, Enoch! Don't be frightened! Stand up and come with me and stand in front of the face of the Lord forever!"[10] And they did.

Many years ago, my beloved friend Helen lost her only child, Phyllis, herself a mother of two young children, to leukemia. Phyllis had waged a courageous battle for life over a period of almost three years. I had been to cemeteries many, many times, all difficult journeys. But this was as lacerating a funeral as I had ever attended. I took Helen's arm as we walked from the car to the gravesite. In a spasm of uncontrollable grief she cried out: "I can't do it, Rabbi, I can't do it! I can't walk to my child's open grave! I can't, I can't, I can't!"

I sought desperately for words that might help, and said, "Helen, the next fifty feet are the hardest you will ever walk in your life. Let's walk them together, and then for you there will be absolutely no mountain you won't be able to climb." The words proved to be fortuitous. Six years ago Helen told me that she had endured and overcome much that would have otherwise been unendurable because, like Jacob, she had wrestled with an angel at her daughter's grave.

Enoch, as told in Genesis, "walked with God," and he was able to do so because the Archangel Gabriel exhorted him to stand on his feet so he could stand up ever after, even in the face of the Ultimate. And it was Gabriel who wrestled with Jacob (see chapter 2) so that Jacob could then stand up to the critical confrontation with his brother, Esau.

## Uriel

~~~~~~~~~~~~~~~~~~~~~~~~~~~~~~~~

Enter Uriel, the last of the archangelic quartet of apocalyptic lore and of the bedtime prayer my father taught me. His name means "God is my light," and as with Michael, Raphael, and Gabriel, the name suits his chief function remarkably well. It has always struck me that the very first words attributed to God are: "Let there be light." That was the primary need when all was in darkness and chaos before the process of the Creation was begun, and light remains the need for all thinking creatures, since chaos still surrounds us and darkness always threatens to enfold us, in life as well as in death.

We want to know what is the purpose of life and to what end have we arrived on this planet, and those are only the mildest of our teleological queries. We have tougher ones. For instance: Is evil so deeply rooted in us that there is no hope for a world without violence and hatred? And the most agitating question of them all: Where is the vaunted God of justice of whom the psalmist proclaimed, "He will rule the world with justice and its people with truth"?

Of all of the books of the Pseudepigrapha demanding that light be shed on these shattering questions, the Fourth Book of Ezra stands out and it is here that the Archangel Uriel plays a starring role.

The biblical Ezra of the Persian period in Jewish history (who lived circa 450 B.C.E.) was given voice by the author of our book, who lived and wrote about the year 100 C.E., thirty years after the destruction of the Second Temple. If the destruction of Solomon's Temple in 586 B.C.E. by the Babylonians triggered serious introspection by the Jewish people and led to such biblical books as Job, Ecclesiastes, and Daniel, the demolition of the Second Temple by the Romans in the year 70 was an even more devastating shock to the national nervous system, as well as to that of the individual Jew, who nonetheless remained committed to the God of his fathers.

After Pompey invaded Jerusalem in 63 B.C.E. the Romans were, in effect, the rulers of the land of Israel and its people. But a succession of insurrections in Judaea and especially in the Galilee infuriated the Romans. Many Jews were put to death by the cruel and uniquely Roman method of crucifixion. The Romans sent procurators to rule Judaea; they overtaxed the people to the point of widespread penury; they offended the Jews' religious sensibilities with their pagan rites; and they reacted to sporadic rebellions with sadistic savagery.

The spirit of national rebellion mounted steadily among an ever larger number of the Jews until it erupted with volcanic force in the year 66. Though the Jews took over full control of Jerusalem, in the end, Generals Vespasian and, later, Titus, his son, laid siege to Jerusalem, broke through the formidable walls, set fire to the Holy Temple, and virtually wiped out the women, men, and children of the city. Victorious Titus marched back to Rome with hundreds of Jewish prisoners bearing the precious Menorahs and other sacred vessels of the Temple on their stooped shoulders. "Judaea Capta!"—the gleeful cry of the Eternal City's populace—became a motto inscribed on Roman coins as well as on a famous tourist site in Italy's capital, the Arch of Titus.

Only an archangel could possibly explain the whys and

wherefore enshrined in the Arch of Titus, the catastrophe that befell the people of God. Only a godly person—one who was the embodiment of unflinching devotion to the law of God, the Torah—could ask why and wherefore.

So enter Uriel and Ezra.

Ezra saw the devastation of Jerusalem at the hands of Babylon (throughout his vision, Babylon stands for Rome):

> My thoughts welled up in my heart because I saw the desolation of Zion and the wealth of those who lived in Babylon . . . Are the deeds of those who inhabit Babylon any better? Is that why she has gained dominion over Zion? For when I came here (to Babylon) I saw ungodly deeds without number, and my soul has seen many sinners during these thirty years. And my heart failed me, for I have seen how you endure those who sin, and have spared those who act wickedly and have destroyed your people and have preserved your enemies and *have not shown to anyone how your way may be comprehended* (italics added).[11]

I was at Auschwitz in the fall of 1945 among a delegation of American Rabbis. Near the entrance of one of the gas chambers there was a fifty-foot mountain of baby shoes, shoes that survived the Holocaust, the shoes of incinerated children aged one to eight or nine: My first vision of Babylon. Those baby shoes have recurred in my nightmares for almost half a century.

So Ezra waits for Uriel's reply to the Jobian questions: What meaning can we find in the cruelty of a world created by a benevolent God who has not shown to anyone how His way may be comprehended? Uriel speaks, but not to the question. The angel of light dispenses a torrent of words, images, and counterquestions, exactly in the mode of God's response to Job out of the whirlwind. God responded to Job with this challenge:

Who is this who darkens council, speaking without knowledge?
Gird your loins like a man;
I will ask and you will inform me.
Where were you when I laid the earth's foundations?
Speak if you have understanding.
Do you know who fixed its dimensions
Or who measured it with a line? . . .
Who closed the sea behind doors
When it pushed forth out of the womb, . . .
When I made breakers My limit for it,
And set up its bar and doors . . .
Have you ever commanded the day to break,
Assigned the dawn its place . . .
Have you penetrated to the sources of the sea,
Or walked in the recesses of the deep? . . .

"Hell no!" is how Job, in effect, responded. "I am not asking to muscle in on your territory, dear Lord. None of the questions you put to me are within my ken. *But hell itself is.* I'm going through it now, right now. There *is* one question among the many you put to me, dear God, that I can answer. You ask:

" 'Have the gates of death been disclosed to you?
Have you seen the gates of deep darkness?' "

(JOB 38:17)

"Hell, yes, I have! Why have You put me through hell or why have You allowed evil people to do so? I am entitled to an answer."

But there is none—not from God to Job and not from Uriel to Ezra. Uriel says:

> "Your understanding has utterly failed regarding this world, and do you think you can comprehend the way of the Most High? . . . I have been sent to show you three problems. If you can solve one of them for me, I also will show you the way you desire to see, and will teach you why the heart is evil . . . Go, weigh for me the weight of fire, or measure for me a blast of wind, or call back for me the day that is past . . ."[12]

The authors of both Job and 4 Ezra were men of brilliant mind and earnest purpose. So have been many contemporary historians, philosophers, sociologists, theologians, and poets who have wrestled with the meaning of the Holocaust and, like Uriel, Archangel of Light, have attempted to supply something for survivors like Ezra to cling to—so that they might not go insane.

But reason, logic, and intelligence are completely beyond the pale of the satanic. It is absurd to try to explain Auschwitz. It is obscene to even pretend to comprehend it. The "why" of it all will ever elude us.

Ezra could not remain silent. His heart enveloped all human pain, even the pain of those who inflicted pain. While he received no satisfactory response to his burning question about the suffering of the innocent, he could not desist from prayer:

> "Be not angry with those who are deemed worse than beasts; but love those who have always put their trust in your glory. For we and our fathers have passed our lives in ways that bring death, but you, because of us sinners, are called merciful . . . For the righteous, who have many works laid up with you, shall receive their reward in consequence of their own deeds. But what is man, that you are angry with him; or what is a mortal race that you are so bitter against it? For in truth there is no one among those who have been born who has not acted wickedly . . . There is no one who has not transgressed. For in this, O Lord, your righteousness and goodness will be declared, when you are merciful to those who have no good works."[13]

How noble Ezra's concern for the unworthy "who have no good works," for the ungodly who have shown no mercy to others. But the Archangel Uriel, speaking in God's name, does not buy into that. Uriel bespeaks the Jewish passion for justice:

> ". . . For this is the way of which Moses, while he was alive, spoke to the people, saying 'Choose for yourself life, that you may live!' But they did not believe him, or the prophets

after him . . . Therefore there shall not be grief at their damnation, so much as joy over those to whom salvation is assured."[14]

God, said both the Scroll people and the Pseudepigraphers, is indeed a God of mercy. But He is the God of justice as well. As the Rabbis of the Talmud defined Him He
appears both as *Elohim*, enthroned upon the seat of Justice, and as *Adonai*, enthroned upon the seat of Mercy. To
pardon persistent evil is to perpetuate it. On the other
hand, to look upon the evildoer without compassion is a
form of blindness not to be attributed to the Almighty.

For evil does and always will exist. God Himself planted
it in the Garden of Eden. He therefore must have a certain
tolerance—and even a purpose—for it. He cannot over-
look the fact that ever since Adam and Eve and Cain and
Abel, the human being has been in unceasing battle with
the Serpent whom both Jewish and Christian tradition
often identify with Satan. Satan is a formidable foe, but
dimly understood. He is, after all, the Prince of Darkness.

So in this very dim period of Jewish history the angels
worked as a bridge between man and a God they could not
understand. And since even the most brilliant scholars and
the most faithful Jews could not provide explanations for
the horrors that befell their people—could not put words
in God's mouth—they provided angels to speak for Him.
But even the angels could not offer adequate reasoning.
Close to God, but also like humans, they understand only
that it is beyond their realm.

CHAPTER 4

~

*Satan*

*and His*

*Angels*

## The Source Material

~ ~ ~ ~ ~ ~ ~ ~ ~ ~ ~ ~ ~ ~ ~ ~ ~ ~ ~ ~ ~ ~ ~ ~ ~

As discussed in chapter 3, the Rabbis of the First and Second Centuries C.E. who edited the Hebrew Bible excluded those Jewish religious writings deemed dangerous

*The Pseudepigrapha, the Talmud and Midrash, and one seminal medieval document were used as sources for this chapter.

to some basic Judaic principles, designating these "outside" works as *apocrypha*. Included within the latter are works described as *pseudepigrapha*. They are writings attributed to famous biblical figures by authors of a much later time in order to enhance reader interest. The treatment of Satan in the Pseudepigrapha may have seemed particularly subversive of Judaic emphasis on the omnipotence of God and on its denial that other celestial forces have the power to oppose Him.

The Talmud, composed over the first five centuries of the Christian era is, after the Hebrew Bible, the pillar upon which Judaism rests. While its basic contents are legal discussions and decisions, it also contains much material of sermonic and legendary nature that is generally centered on the interpretation of passages in the Hebrew Bible. This latter material is called Midrash. Compilations of Midrash out of the Talmud and other sources were made mainly from the fifth through the twelfth centuries and constitute invaluable sources for Jewish lore and outlook upon an immense number of the problems of life and the destiny of both the Jewish people and of humanity as a whole.

The books from the Hebrew Bible used in this chapter are Genesis, especially chapter 6, which deals with fallen angels; Exodus, which inspired a Midrash about Satan's role in the episode of the Golden Calf; Isaiah, about a prophet of the eighth century B.C.E., whose fourteenth chapter evoked applications to an arrogant and rebellious Satan; Ezekiel, about a prophet of the sixth century B.C.E.

whose mystic visions abounded in celestial beings; Job, possibly composed in the third or fourth century B.C.E., in which Satan appears as an adversary of humans; Daniel, composed during the Maccabean Revolt, 175–164 B.C.E., whose apocalyptic visions are germane to the material of this chapter; and the Psalms, devotional poetry composed over hundreds of years from the time of King David, 1000 B.C.E., and possibly to as late as 200 B.C.E. (the fear of death finds frequent voice in the Psalms and bears a relationship to the role of Satan as the Angel of Death, developed in later generations).

The books of the Pseudepigrapha from which material relevant to Satan has been drawn are 1 Enoch and 2 Enoch, the Martyrdom and Ascension of Isaiah, and the Life of Adam and Eve, each of which offers its own version of the behavior of Satan and his angels that led to their fall from heaven and the grace of God.

The *Alphabet of Ben Sira* was probably composed in the ninth or tenth century and contains a listing of humans who defied the Angel of Death, alias Satan, and who reached heaven without prior loss of life.

## Satan and Job

∾ ∾ ∾ ∾ ∾ ∾ ∾ ∾ ∾ ∾ ∾ ∾ ∾ ∾ ∾ ∾ ∾ ∾ ∾ ∾

Satan has a bad reputation as the incarnation of evil, sin, temptation—hell itself. Satan is the antagonist of God, pitting his hateful nature against the loving Deity—even plotting to unseat the Lord and to occupy His throne.

That's a heavy load to carry, especially given that Satan is a law-abiding citizen of the Angelic Host, an agent of God who goes about doing his job as faithfully as he knows how. What is his job? It is to look into the behavior of human beings and to report back to his divine employer any wayward deeds and aberrations he can discover. He is the celestial prosecuting attorney who gathers his evidence carefully and sets it before the Supreme Judge.

As a distinct angelic persona, rather than as a generic Hebrew term for "adversary," Satan first appeared in the prologue to the Book of Job:

> One day the divine beings presented themselves before the Lord and Satan came along with them. The Lord said to Satan: "Where have you been?" Satan answered the Lord: "I have been roaming all over the earth." The Lord said to Satan, "Have you noticed My servant Job? There is no one like him on earth, a blameless and upright man who fears God and shuns evil!" Satan answered the Lord, "Does Job not have good reason to fear God? Why it is You who have fenced him round, him and his household and all that he has. You have blessed his efforts so that his possessions spread out in the land. But lay your hand upon all that he has and he will surely blaspheme You to Your face." The Lord replied to Satan, "See, all that he has is in your power; only do not lay a hand on him." Satan departed from the presence of the Lord.
>
> (JOB 1:1–12)

Satan did his work thoroughly, and as a result, Job became an impoverished and childless man. But he still remained faithful to God, saying: "The Lord has given and the Lord has taken away; blessed be the name of the Lord." At the next heavenly conference, God taunts Satan:

> "Have you noticed my servant Job? There is no one like him on earth, a blameless and upright man who fears God and shuns evil. He still keeps his integrity; so you have incited Me against him to destroy him for no good reason."
>
> (JOB 2:3)

But Satan persists, saying that as long as Job is not afflicted in his own body, he will retain his righteousness. With God's permission Satan then inflicts "a severe inflammation on Job from the sole of his foot to the crown of his head." Miserable Job seats himself on a pile of ashes, scratching his itching skin with a broken potsherd.

> His wife said to him, "You still keep your integrity! Curse God and die!" But he said to her . . . "Should we accept only good from God and not accept evil?" For all that, Job said nothing sinful.
>
> (JOB 3:9, 10)

From the above-cited passages, we learn some important notions as to the functions of Satan in the tradition of the Hebrew Bible. Satan has no authority to initiate any action without the permission of God. His methodology is entrapment—a legal procedure authorized by the highest court. Further, nothing in the text suggests that Satan takes delight in what he is doing. Satan's prerogative remains limited in the Hebrew Bible and even at that derives only from God.

## Satan and the Fallen Angels

In the pseudepigraphic literature, Satan begins the transformation that cast him in the role of God's adversary, ultimately as His antithesis, and in Christianity as the Antichrist. This process of transformation has its roots in the Book of Genesis, chapter 6, verses 1 through 7, in as enigmatic a passage as one may find in the Hebrew Bible:

> When men began to increase on earth and daughters were born to them, the divine beings saw how beautiful the daughters of men were and took wives from among those that pleased them. The Lord said, "My breath shall not abide in man forever, since he too is flesh; let the days allowed him be one hundred and twenty years." It was then, and later too, that the Nephilim appeared on earth—when the divine beings cohabited with the daughters of men, who bore them offspring. They were the heroes of old, the men of renown.

> The Lord saw how great was man's wickedness on earth, and how every plan devised by his mind was nothing but evil all the time. And the Lord regretted that He had made man on earth, His heart was saddened.
>
> (GENESIS 6:1–7)

The above account seems to be a fragment of a much fuller story known to its author that was probably heavily censored. It evokes some ancient myth about divine beings who had sexual intercourse with mortal women, who in turn produced prodigies of some kind—giants, "heroes," or "men of renown."

Who are the divine beings in Genesis 6? If angels, since when did they come to possess a sexual drive? Were their marriages to mortal women forbidden? If so, why doesn't our text say so? Was the "wickedness of man on earth" connected with this union of "divine beings" with human females? If so, how or why? If God is all-knowing, how could He not have anticipated all of this when He created Adam and Eve and His armies of heavenly angels?

The author of this story in Genesis may well have been recording an unsavory bit of his people's folklore that is inconsistent with the doctrines of Mosaic monotheism. "Divine beings," to begin with, are incompatible with the idea of One God. To the extent that angels were messengers of God, they could fit into the mosaic of the Jewish biblical tradition. However, angels, acting upon their own initiative and succumbing to their own desires, are an alien element in the Hebrew Bible, as has just been demonstrated even with the angel named Satan.

The word *Nephilim* in the Genesis passage is somewhat obscure. Elsewhere in the Pentateuch they seem to be synonymous with giants. Still, the root of *Nephilim* in Hebrew means "to fall," and the concept of Fallen Angels was common to all Semitic peoples. Usually these were gods or demons who rebelled against a chief deity and were cast out of its presence only to reappear among mortals as malevolent incubi of one form or another—satans, devils, imps, monsters, and other evil things.

Not surprisingly, the first full account of the Fallen Angels is in the Pseudepigrapha. The people who wrote its various books were wrestling with the problems of ongoing Jewish catastrophes and were especially anxious to vindicate the God of Israel by disassociating Him from the evil that men do. So they simply shifted the responsibility to other shoulders. The myth of the Fallen Angels suited this purpose remarkably well, beginning with chapter 6 of 1 Enoch:

> In those days, when the children of men had multiplied, it happened that there were born unto them handsome and beautiful daughters. And the angels, the children of heaven, saw them and desired them; and they said to one another, "Come let us choose wives for ourselves among the daughters of man and beget us children." And Semyaza, being

their leader, said unto them, "I fear that perhaps you will not consent that this deed should be done, and I alone will become responsible for this great sin" . . . Then they all swore together and bound one another by the curse. And they descended in the days of Jared[1] on the summit of Mount Hermon.[2] . . .

And they took wives unto themselves, and everyone chose one woman for himself, and they began to go unto them. And they taught them magical medicine, incantations, the cutting of roots . . . And the women became pregnant and gave birth to great giants whose heights were three hundred cubits. These giants consumed the produce of all the people until the people detested feeding them. So the giants turned against the people and began to eat them. And they began to sin against birds, wild beasts, reptiles and fish. And their flesh was devoured the one by the other, and they drank blood. And then the earth brought an accusation against the oppressors.

And Azazel taught the people the art of making swords and knives and shields . . . And there were many wicked ones and they committed adultery and sinned, and all their conduct became corrupt . . .[3]

The darkly mysterious passage of Genesis 6 is suddenly illuminated (with a vengeance) in 1 Enoch 6! Things begin to fit together. A bad lot of angels are sexually aroused by ravishing human females. They know that as angels— purely spiritual beings—they may not have intercourse with women/humans, but they commit the foul deed anyway. They lead humankind astray and, before long, the earth with its people and flora and fauna is a cesspool of gore and degeneracy.

At this point, the good Archangels Michael, Uriel, Raphael, and Gabriel report this outrageous development to God and plead for justice and the end of evil. God accedes to the plea and promises in due course to wipe injustice from the face of the earth and to sow the everlasting seeds of righteousness and truth.

> And all the children of the people will become righteous, and all nations shall worship and bless Me . . . And the earth shall be cleansed from all pollution, and from all sin, and from all plague, and from all suffering . . . And peace and truth shall become partners together in all the days of the world, and in all the generations of the world.[4]

As to the rebellious and fallen angels "who have abandoned the high heaven, the holy eternal place," they would have neither forgiveness nor peace because they relished violence and reveled in murder.

An apocryphal vision unfolds of the ultimate triumph of God's good over the evil forces that launched an invasion of earth from their heavenly base.

God has not disappeared; that was the message of the author of 1 Enoch to his fellow Jews of the first century B.C.E. Our suffering stems from the corruption introduced into the world by the progeny of rebellious Fallen Angels.

While sexual lust is at the root of the Fallen Angels episode in 1 Enoch, another version is found in 2 Enoch, which scholars also call the "Slavonic" Enoch. Here Satan himself appears as the culprit, but it is the lust for *power* that casts Satan down from heaven:

> Here Satan[ail] was hurled from the heights, together with his angels. But one from the order of the archangels deviated, together with the division that was under his authority. He thought up the impossible idea that he might place his throne higher than the clouds which are above the earth, and that he might become equal to my power. And I (i.e., God) hurled him out from the height, together with his angels. And he was flying around in the air, ceaselessly, above the Bottomless.[5]

Satan, the arrogant rebel who challenges God Himself, is now seen as the demonic force who inspires the abandonment of the service of God in humankind. Satan thereby sets up his own kingdom in an attempt to compete with God for the souls of men. The chronicler of the biblical books of 1 Kings and 2 Kings does indeed divide the monarchs of Judah and Israel into two categories: those like David, who did what is right in the eyes of the Lord, and those like Jeroboam, who did what was evil in God's eyes. These last worshiped the idols of the peoples surrounding them. But it is never suggested that they were anything *but* idols, without real power.

# Satan and King Manasseh

≈ ≈ ≈ ≈ ≈ ≈ ≈ ≈ ≈ ≈ ≈ ≈ ≈ ≈ ≈ ≈ ≈ ≈ ≈ ≈

The worst of all the kings who did evil was Manasseh (692–638 B.C.E.), whose long reign was an uninterrupted nightmare of apostasy, corruption, and violence. In 2 Kings, chapter 21: "Manasseh put so many innocent persons to death that he filled Jerusalem with blood from end to end . . ."

But while the biblical historian viewed Manasseh as self-deluded, the author of the Martyrdom and Ascension of Isaiah, a book of the Pseudepigrapha (dating most probably to the middle of the first century C.E.) wrote:

> And it came about that after Hezekiah had died, and Manasseh had become King, Manasseh did not remember the commands of Hezekiah his father, but forgot them; and Samael (Satan) dwelt in Manasseh and clung closely to him. And Manasseh abandoned the service of the Lord of his father and he served Satan, and his angels and his powers . . . And he turned his father's house . . . away from the service of the Lord. Manasseh turned them away so that they served Beliar [another of Satan's names]; for the angel of iniquity who rules this world is Beliar.[6]

At a time when the Jews were besieged by the Romans and flooded with trouble, this pseudepigraphic author affirmed that it was Satan/Samael/Beliar who was in control of the world. But it was the sin of those who succumbed to the blandishments of Satan that gave him sovereignty. Satan rules by neither justice nor mercy. As suffering Job put it:

> "The earth is handed over to the wicked one;
> He covers the eyes of judges.
> If it is not He, then who?"

Job, antidualist that he was, could not conceive of anyone other than God ruling the world, and in that case God was responsible for *everything*, including evil. Not so the pseudepigraphers. As matters stood in their corrupted surroundings, they insisted that Satan—a separate being—was responsible for their suffering.

YET A THIRD motive for the aberrant behavior of the Fallen Angels is supplied in another book of Pseudepigrapha, the Life of Adam and Eve, whose likely date of composition was the first century C.E. It relates some episodes in the lives of the first humans after their expulsion from the Garden of Eden, especially their deathbed memories and the moral to be drawn from them.

In this version of the Fallen Angels tale, Satan emerges as an all-too-human angel. When Adam was created (so Life of Adam and Eve relates), Satan refused to bow down before him despite the Archangel Michael's command that the entire angelic host do so, inasmuch as Adam had been made in the image of God. Defiantly, Satan said: "I do not worship Adam . . . I will not worship one inferior and subsequent to me." Satan then became the ringleader of other rebellious angels who also refused to prostrate themselves before Adam. For such insubordination, Satan and his company were cast out of heaven onto the earth. Satan regarded Adam as the source of this calamity and wreaked his vengeance by assuming the form of the Serpent, seducing Eve into sin, and then deriving satisfaction from seeing both Eve and Adam expelled from the Garden of Eden, much as he had been ousted from heaven.

## The Original Sin: Two Views

~ ~ ~ ~ ~ ~ ~ ~ ~ ~ ~ ~ ~ ~ ~ ~ ~ ~ ~ ~ ~

Classic Christian teaching places a huge emphasis upon the errant action of Adam and Eve in tasting the Forbidden Fruit. It has been designated as the Original Sin and is basic to Christian theology. By permitting themselves to be seduced by Satan contrary to God's specific instructions, Adam and Eve and all their descendants became tainted by that sin and were condemned to eternal damnation. Were it not for God's love, man would be incapable by his own deeds—no matter what they are—of being reintroduced into God's grace and thereby achieving salvation. Christianity's greatest teacher, Saint Paul, emphasized constantly that salvation is not possible by "works" alone. The "works," or commandments prescribed by the Law of Moses (the Torah), failed to bring about human reconciliation with God, Paul claimed. But God so loved humanity that He sent His only begotten Son to earth to die as the sacrificial lamb for the sins of all who accept Him (the Son) as their savior. "Believe in the Lord Jesus Christ and ye shall be saved." Those who remain unbelievers are held in Satan's clutches.

Judaism has flatly rejected the notions that sin is genetically transmitted; that Adam and Eve's sin was irredeemable; that damnation awaits those who cannot and will not conceive of a God become human, any more than they can conceive of a human become God; and that human mischief is the fault of an independent Satan acting against the will of God.

According to Jewish tradition, the sin of Adam and Eve was not transmitted to their descendants, therefore each person can still cultivate his own paradise as long as he avoids the Serpent.

## Fear of the Angel of Death

~ ~ ~ ~ ~ ~ ~ ~ ~ ~ ~ ~ ~ ~ ~ ~ ~ ~ ~ ~ ~

There is, however, no avoiding death. "It is the lot of all flesh," says the apocryphal Book of Ben Sira. According to ancient Jewish folklore, embodied in the Midrash (sermonic elaborations upon biblical texts), after Adam had disobeyed God, the Almighty delivered the whole of the animal world into the power of the Angel of Death. Death is our destiny, no matter who we are or think we are. King Solomon, the wisest of men, once discovered a lifelike statue of impressive and imperious demeanor. On it was a silver plate inscribed in Greek with the following words:

> I, Shadad ben Ad, ruled over a thousand thousand provinces, rode on a thousand thousand horses, had a thousand thousand kings under me, and slew a thousand thousand heroes, and when the Angel of Death approached me, I was powerless.[7]

This legend tallies with countless passages in Jewish lore that deal with death as personified by the angel charged with bringing it about. One statement from the Midrash is especially terse: "On the very first day God created the Angel of Death, for it is written: 'And darkness was on the face of the deep.' Darkness is the Angel of Death who blackens the faces of human beings with dread."

But the Angel of Death does not turn back when our time has come, not even for King David, as explained in this legend from the Midrash:

> King David asked the Lord, blessed be He, to tell him how long he would live. And the Lord, blessed be He, answered: "I never tell it to a human being, for I have taken an oath never to reveal it to any man." Then King David said, "Tell

me at least on what day I am to die." Then the Lord, blessed be He, told him, "It will be on a Sabbath." King David again asked, "Let me die on a Sunday." (So as not to mar the peace and joy of Sabbath). Then the Lord, blessed be He, said: "No, for the reign of your son is to begin on Sunday, and the Kingdom of the one must not overlap that of the other even for one second." Then King David studied (the Torah) the whole day long every Sabbath so that the Angel of Death should not be able to touch him. On the Sabbath on which he was to die, the Angel of Death came and wanted to take his soul, but David was poring over a book without interrupting his study. Hence the Angel of Death could do nothing to him. Then the Angel of Death thought to himself: "How can I take his soul? For as long as he is engaged in study, I cannot touch him." Now King David had a beautiful pleasure garden behind his house. So the Angel of Death went into the garden and shook the trees. King David wanted to see who was there among his trees. And he went up a ladder, it broke under him and he stopped studying, whereupon the Angel of Death took his life, and he earned a seat in Paradise.[8]

This tale has much to say about life and death. First, consciously or subconsciously, we do think about death. We wonder when our time will come and we bargain—with ourselves and with God—for just a little more time, if only one more day. Second, as long as we are occupied with the good and the useful, life is very much worth its problems, pangs, and pains. Third, and most subtly, we are reminded of the "beautiful pleasure garden" Adam and Eve called home before the Serpent (alias Satan, alias Samael, alias the

Angel of Death) shook the Tree of Knowledge of Good and Bad and brought down its Forbidden Fruit, thus bringing down death upon Adam and Eve and their progeny.

THE ANGEL OF Death comes to kings and commoners alike. But Jewish lore tells of one human being who, while not able to escape death itself, succeeded in fending off death's ubiquitous messenger. No mere agent of God could take his life. In the end God Himself had to do it, for through the ages the person involved was considered *ish ha-elohim*, the "Man of God." He was Moses.

Forty years in the wilderness followed the Exodus of the Children of Israel from Egypt. It was Moses who led them out, who gave them the word of the One God at Mount Sinai, who was a constant target for the malcontents and mean-spirited among his people. It was Moses who brought his people to the borders of their Promised Land.

At this very moment of a mission nearly accomplished, Moses is informed by God that he is to die on the other side of the River Jordan, and that Joshua would be the man to lead the people into Canaan. In the Hebrew Bible (Numbers 20:22), Moses offers not a word of protest. But the Rabbis, whose sermonic commentaries on the biblical text constitute the literature of Midrash, could not but express their frustration at the unfairness of it all. They recounted stories in which Moses argues boldly against God's verdict and seeks its revocation or, at least, its postponement. God is not moved. He calls first upon the Archangel Gabriel to fetch the soul of Moses. But Gabriel pleads with God to be excused from so painful a task. Then Archangel Michael is asked to do it. He, too, begs off, as does the Angel Zagzagel. Without his being asked, Samael (Satan) volunteers eagerly to fetch the soul of Moses. God is none too anxious to send his usual messenger of death. But Samael's persistence is finally accorded divine consent.

But even Samael is overwhelmed by the radiance and power of the Man of God. He tries again and again to complete his mission. In the end he breaks down in hysteria and returns to God empty-handed.

God is furious. "Go fetch Me Moses' soul, for if you do not do so, I will discharge you from your office of taking men's souls, and appoint another to do it." "O Lord of the world," Samael cries out, "order me to Gehenna [hell] to turn it upside down and I will do it without a moment's hesitation, but I cannot appear before Moses!" This time it is God Who insists that Samael return to earth and come back with Moses' soul.

> When Moses perceived him he arose in anger, and, staff in hand . . . set about to drive Samael away. Samael fled in fear, but Moses pursued him, and when he reached him, he struck him with his staff . . . He was not far from killing him, but a voice resounded from heaven and said: "Let him live, Moses, for the world is in need of him."

To Jewish teaching, the Angel of Death is an integral part of the rhythms of nature, its decay and growth, its darkness and light.

Ultimately God descended from heaven in the company of the Archangels Michael, Gabriel, and Zagzagel, and He took the soul of Moses and superintended his physical burial at the hands of the three angels.

So the Hebrew Bible accepted death as the destiny of all flesh. The belief in a life after death began only in postbiblical literature, either in the form of the immortality of the human soul or, more radically, in the resurrection of the dead who had led worthy lives. The last verses of the Book of Daniel hint of a resurrection at some future Day of Judgment. The Rabbis of the Talmud ultimately elevated belief in resurrection as a basic element of the Jewish faith and, indeed, incorporated it into the very heart of the liturgy known as the Eighteen Benedictions (*Shmoneh Esrai*). The recognized teachers of Judaism sensed a deep need for this new article of faith in a world that saw the Jews bereft of their Holy Temple and deprived of sovereignty over their Holy Land. Even so, the legitimacy of the sovereignty of the Angel of Death continued to be accepted as the necessary governance in the temporal world. "Let him live, Moses, for the world is in need of him" was an exhortation the Jews understood at all times of their history.

≈ ≈ ≈

THE ANGEL OF Death is not expressly mentioned in the Hebrew Bible, although there are a number of passages in which death itself seems to be personified.

But in the immediate pre-Christian era and for a thousand years thereafter, very specific physical descriptions of the Angel of Death are commonplace in Jewish literature. His dimensions, for one, are formidable, reaching from one end of the world to the other. He is all fire, and appears to human sight as if he were full of eyes (reminiscent of the creatures of the prophet Ezekiel's vision who were "full of eyes round about" [Ezekiel 1:18]). He appears in any disguise he chooses to assume, even as an Angel of Light. He often takes on the form of a bird with twelve wings. He carries a sword as the trademark of his vocation. At the moment of a human's death, he stands at the head of the dying with his sword unsheathed, a bitter drop clinging to the metal. The dying person sees the Angel of Death, is seized by convulsions of terror, and begins to gasp. At that moment the Angel of Death shakes the drop into the person's open mouth and it is all over.

The poisonous and fatal drop is advanced by some scholars as an explanation for the derivation of Samael, one of the names of the Angel of Death. *Sam* in Hebrew means "poison," so that Samael might well mean "The Supreme Poison." Two other etymologies are advanced by scholars. The first would derive Samael from the Hebrew *Smol*, which means "left side," traditionally the site of the Evil Inclination *(Yetzer ha-Ra)* within human beings—the

Good Inclination *(Yetzer-tov)* being located on the right side. The second associates Samael with the Hebrew verb *samay*, which means "to blind." All three etymologies are, in fact, true to the Judaic conception of Satan. The Babylonian Talmud, consisting of the teaching of the Rabbis from about 200 to 500 C.E., contains a statement attributed to the third-century sage Simeon ben Lakish:

> "Satan, the Evil Inclination and the Angel of Death are one and the same."

## Satan's Corrupted Nature

Throughout the Satan-Samael narratives in the literature of the Jews, the theme of temptation as a main source of evil and corruption dominates. Temptation appears in many forms: greed, lust, jealousy, ambition, and an excessive appetite for almost anything dangled before human eyes. The poisoning of our waters, the pollution of our air, the carnage of our wars—all of these trace back to a potential paradise that has been lost to the enticements of the Satan/Samael/Serpent.

Satan turns human beings away from the path of righteousness (the root word in Hebrew, *Satoh*, means "to divert, to turn away"). It is, in fact, the Evil Inclination within each of us that leads us off the straight and narrow.

Satan is, of course, the catalyst for the supreme sin of the Children of Israel on their way to the Promised Land. In the third month following their Exodus from Egypt, they arrived at Mount Sinai in the wilderness. Moses ascended the mountain, and from its peak, enveloped in clouds, came forth the voice of God Himself, pronouncing the Ten Commandments, which begin with the words:

> "I the Lord am your God who brought you out of the land of Egypt, the house of bondage. You shall have no other gods beside Me. You shall not make for yourself a graven image, or any likeness of what is in the heaven above, or on the earth below, or in the waters under the earth. You shall not bow down to them or serve them."
>
> (EXODUS 20:2-5)

Moses was to spend forty days and nights in proximity to God while the rest of the laws of the Torah were being given to him for transmittal to the Children of Israel. He had to overcome strong angelic opposition to his very presence in the higher spheres: "What business does one who was born of woman have among us?" they all demanded. God had to persuade the angels that the Torah that Moses had come to receive was not designed for sinless, aerial creatures. It was man who needed its laws and strictures, for man was prone to sin because of the Evil Inclination. As if to prove it, the Children of Israel were on the verge of committing the most grievous of sins as the fateful forty days were nearing their end. They had become impatient waiting for the great leader to return, and convinced themselves that he never would. So they demanded of Aaron, their high priest and the older brother of Moses, to fashion a molten god for them, to whom they could turn for protection. Aaron tried to put them off as best he could:

> But at noon on the fortieth day Satan came, and by a feat of magic, conjured up for the people a vision of Moses lying stretched out dead on a bier that floated midway between earth and heaven. Pointing to it with their fingers, they cried: "This is the man Moses that brought us up out of the land of Egypt."[9]

There followed the making of the Golden Calf, before which most of the Children of Israel prostrated themselves in adoration, to their shame and disgrace, not to mention the displeasure of the Lord and the heartbreak of Moses himself (see Exodus 32). It was also a high point in Satan's career. It had been a long, long time since he had caused Adam and Eve to stumble on the rocks of the primeval Garden of Eden. Now he had engineered the stumbling of an entire people on the rocks of the Sinai wilderness.

≈ ≈ ≈

# Is Satan Necessary?

If the Jewish tradition never regarded Satan as a rival of God or independent of His will, why does he exist at all? All that has been written to this point should contribute toward an answer to the question.

The Hebrew word *Satan* means "adversary"—not of God but of humankind. The Judaic conceptions of God's omnipotence and absolute unity allow for no adversary in His domain. But God created humans and granted them free will. And He endowed them with the capacity for both good and evil.

*The Serpent in the Garden of Eden is the Satan within us.* He is the architect of our pernicious behavior, the tireless seducer, the rationalizer of evil, and the agent of our own undoing. But he *can* be resisted successfully. The antidote to his poison is the firm belief that his role is to put our souls through his temptations. In that sense God intended Satan to fashion our moral character.

Judaism firmly believes that ample precedent had been provided by its biblical and Talmudic ancestors for triumph over Satan. Abraham, Isaac, Jacob, Joseph, Moses, Aaron, and David all succeeded in facing down Satan. So did all who are called *tsadikkim* ("the righteous"). None of the above giants was without human frailties. None was invulnerable to sin. Yet all overcame their flaws by rising above them over the body of a vanquished Satan-within. In doing so, they achieved greater proximity to their unchallenged Creator. That, in the eyes of the Jewish tradition, is the ultimate, most desirable goal of a human life.

# A Registry of Immortals

~~~~~~~~~~~~~~~~~~~~~~~~~~~~~~~~~

In exceptional situations, God Himself—the Rock of Israel, as He is so often designated in Jewish liturgy—snatches some special humans from the clutches of Satan/Samael/the Angel of Death. In a medieval Jewish Midrash designated as *Alphabetum Siracidis* by the brilliant nineteenth-century bibliographer Moritz Steinschneider, a registry of immortals is included, people who were admitted to paradise without ever crossing the bridge of death. They are:

Enoch, who "walked with God; then he was no more, for God took him."

Eleazer, the pagan servant of Abraham, who was the first convert to the God of his master.

Serach, the daughter of Asher, one of Jacob's twelve sons, because she brought the news to the Patriarch that his favorite son, Joseph, was still alive after Jacob had long thought him dead. Serach was told by Jacob: "The mouth that has conveyed such good tidings shall not taste death."

Bithya, daughter of Pharaoh, who had the infant Moses

fetched from the wicker basket floating on the Nile and reared him to maturity as his foster mother.

Ebed-Melech, the Ethiopian who risked his life to save the prophet Jeremiah from the pit into which he had been thrown by the men of King Zedekiah and where he would otherwise have died (see Jeremiah 38).

The servant of Rabbi Judah, the Prince (circa 200 C.E.), because he was righteous, gentle, and humble.

Jabez, who in the Syriac Apocalypse of Baruch is mentioned among the saintly leaders of the people at the time of the destruction of the First Temple (586 B.C.E.).

Rabbi Joshua ben Levi, a legendary Talmudic figure who lived early in the third century in Lod, Palestine, and who is reported to have had a personal encounter with the prophet Elijah.

Hiram, King of Tyre, who supplied the materials and the workers for the building of Solomon's Temple.

The entire family of Jonadab ben Rechab, who is singled out in 2 Kings as a man of unblemished piety in an impious generation, and of whom Jeremiah said:

> "Thus said the Lord of Hosts, the God of Israel: 'Because you have obeyed the charge of your ancestor Jonadab and kept all his commandments, and done all that he enjoined upon you . . . There shall never cease to be a man of the line of Jonadab son of Rechab, standing before Me.' "
>
> (JEREMIAH 35:18, 19)

Finally, the bird Milcham, who, alone in the animal kingdom, resisted Eve's blandishments and heeded God's command not to eat of the Tree of Knowledge of Good and Bad. An old Midrash has God denying the Angel of Death jurisdiction over this most righteous of birds:

> "I will raise him up forever and ever as an example to mankind; he and his posterity shall in future bear testimony to the merit of Israel . . . When he attains to the age of a thousand years, he begins to gradually diminish in size until he becomes like a little bird and then his strength is renewed like the eagle, so that he never wholly dies."
>
> (*ALPHABETUM SIRACIDIS*)

In a somewhat different version of Midrash (Bereshith Rabba 19:5), the bird is called *Khol* (or "phoenix"). He lives to be a thousand. Then a fire breaks out in his nest, destroying it and leaving only a small residue the size of an egg, from which the phoenix is reborn to live a thousand years more. And the process is repeated.

The activity of the Angel of Death of whatever appellation comes full cycle with the immortality of the phoenix. Satan had no power over the phoenix because that bird had not been traduced by Satan, because he had resisted the lure of the forbidden fruit and therefore death and its messenger could not touch him.

But there is something deeper in the legend of the phoenix. The life of the bird is endless—not painless, and not free of disasters. His nest is regularly engulfed in flames.

But there is always the saving remnant, the surviving egg of that holocaust. Like the Burning Bush beheld by Moses, it refuses to be consumed. Often in the Talmud and Midrash, the Jewish people are compared to a bird. Undoubtedly, the sages of the Jewish people from the time of the burning of the First Temple by Nebuchadnezzar of Babylon; through the incineration of the Second Temple by Titus; and on through the disasters of the Crusades; the expulsions from England, France, and Spain in the late Middle Ages; the Chmielnicki Massacres of 1648–1649 in Poland; the tsarist pogroms; the Soviet terrors; and the fire of all fires—the Holocaust, saw the phoenix as the apotheosis of the Jewish people—a standing, living symbol of the limits and limitations of the Angel of Death.

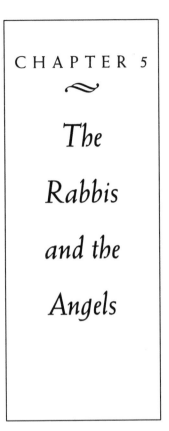

CHAPTER 5

~

## *The Rabbis and the Angels*

## The Talmud

~~~~~~~~~~~~~~~~~~~~~~~~~~~~~~~~~

Second in importance only to the Hebrew Bible itself is the Talmud. It was developed over a period of some five hundred years with the participation of a thousand scholars of Jewish law and transmitters of Jewish lore. They lived mostly in Palestine and Babylonia (today's Iraq) and their intellectual activity unfolded in both countries mainly during the first five centuries of the Christian era. Up to about the year 200, Palestine was the center and fountainhead of Jewish life, no matter where else Jews lived. Despite the destruction of the Second Temple during the war of Judea against Rome (66–70 C.E.), and despite the Bar Cokhba Revolt (another major attempt by the Jews to shake off the Roman yoke [132–135 C.E.] with its attendant disaster of 585,000 Jewish dead and a land laid waste), Jewish spiritual life in the Holy Land continued in the Galilee. There the descendants of Hillel, the great Rabbi of the early first century who became *Nassi* (spiritual head) of the Jews, continued the tradition of fruitful religious teaching that culminated in the Mishnah, the first comprehensive code of Jewish law since the codes of the Hebrew Bible.

This was accomplished under the editorship of Hillel's great-great-grandson, Rabbi Judah Hanassi, about the year 200. Shortly thereafter, the fulcrum of Jewish life shifted to Babylonia, where first under the Parthians and then under the Sassanids the Jews developed one of the strongest diaspora communities of their history. Great academies of learning were established in Sura and Pumbedita in which leading masters, using the Mishnah as their basic text, debated, discussed, and elaborated principles of Jewish laws and belief, ethical guidelines, legendary materials, folk wisdom, and a dizzying array of subjects having to do with the way a Jew should conduct his life, the way in which he should walk (*Halakah*, the generic Hebrew term for religious law, literally means "the way to go").

All of these discussions were recorded at the academies by diligent students. Toward the middle of the fifth century these notes were edited by Rav Ashi and his star pupil Rabbina into the Gemara. The Gemara text was appended to the Mishnah, and the whole is called the Talmud. Since its creation, the Talmud has towered in both the background and foreground of Jewish life.[1]

It should come as no surprise that the subject of angels occupies some space in this magnum opus. The Rabbis of the Talmud could not avoid a theme that had become widespread among the people as a result of their tragic experiences, as well as from the obsessive preoccupation with angels that marked the writings of the Apocrypha, Pseudepigrapha, Dead Sea Scrolls, and emergent christological literature.

## Putting Angels in Their Place

≈ ≈ ≈ ≈ ≈ ≈ ≈ ≈ ≈ ≈ ≈ ≈ ≈ ≈ ≈ ≈ ≈ ≈ ≈ ≈ ≈ ≈

The monotheistic faith founded by Moses about 1300 B.C.E. struggled against pagan culture for over one and a half millennia. It had to wage its battle both within and without. The biblical books of Judges, Samuel, and Kings afford ample evidence of wayward, idolatrous practices by the Jews themselves. The gods of Canaanite civilization were frequently worshiped by the descendants of the Patriarchs. It was not until after the Babylonian exile that monotheism became the unchallenged faith of all the Jews. Then it was their task to fend off the pagan practices of the Persians, Greeks, and Romans who took turns in dominion over the Jewish people. Particularly odious to the Jews was the assumption of divine titles by demented rulers, such as the Roman Emperor Caligula, for example. Basing their reaction to royal arrogation and arrogance upon the biblical Nimrod, who was the "first man of might on earth," and whose kingdom ranged over "Babylon, Erech, Accad, and Calneh" (Genesis 10:8–10), the Rabbis wove a fascinating tale of confrontation between Nimrod, a tyrant who demanded to be worshiped, and Abraham, who, being the first to recognize the one universal God, was the ancestor of the Jews. Abraham's iconoclastic activities (smashing of idols) were subversive in the eyes of Nimrod, who had Abraham imprisoned without food or water for a full year, during which the Archangel Gabriel was sent by God to provide the nourishment necessary for Abraham's survival. Nevertheless, Nimrod decided that his reign of idolatry and brute force could not long survive Abraham's courageous defiance. So he had an enormous fire built, for the stoking of whose flames he ordered everyone of his people to contribute wood. Some of his people had already begun to chant: "The Eternal He is God, the God of the whole world, including the blasphemer Nimrod." This hinted at possible marches on Nimrod's capital of Nineveh; it was, as he saw it, a heresy that had to be incinerated.

As Abraham was about to be catapulted into the fire, Satan, disguised as a human, appeared to him and said: "If you desire to be delivered from the fire of Nimrod, bow down before him and believe in him." But Abraham remained adamant. Though his mother pleaded with him to recant and save his life, he told her: "O mother, water can extinguish Nimrod's fire, but the fire of God will never die out."

> When the angels received the Divine permission to save him, and Gabriel approached him, and asked: "Abraham, shall I save you from the fire?" he replied, "God in whom I trust, the God of heaven and earth, will rescue me." God, seeing the submissive spirit of Abraham, commanded the fire, "Cool down and bring tranquility to my servant Abraham."[2]

In another version of the story (Talmud, Pesahim 118), the Archangel Gabriel seeks God's permission to save Abraham from the fiery furnace. God answers:

> "I am One in my universe and Abraham is One on earth. It is only proper that the One save the One."

The sages of the Talmud understood only too well the dilemma of the dissenter in a camp equipped with the per-

*The Three Men in the Fiery Furnace*

suasive weapons of the gulag and the furnace. The Jews of
the Roman Empire, horrified that the Emperor put statues
within their temples, sent a delegation to Caligula headed
by Philo of Alexandria to protest the wanton trampling of

*The Rabbis and the Angels* ~ 133

Jewish ideals and Jewish conscience. These Jews were openly speaking out against Nimrod, unafraid of the possible consequences.

In the wake of the failed Bar Cokhba Revolt, the Emperor Hadrian issued laws designed to destroy the Jewish faith. One of them was that the Torah might not be taught or studied or written. Violators would incur the death penalty. Ten great Rabbis were caught in the act of teaching Torah. Every one of them was put to death in savage ways —including the greatest Rabbi of them all, Rabbi Akiba, who was flayed and skinned alive. As death came near, his anguished pupils saw him smiling and asked, "How can you smile at such a moment, Rabbi?" He answered: "All of my life I have been praying the words: 'Love the Lord your God with all your heart, and with all your soul, and with all your might.' I have long wondered: could I love my God even when He allows my life to be forced from me? I now know the answer." The Talmudic legend concludes that the smile continued through Akiba's last words: "Hear, O Israel, the Lord alone is our God."

At a time of the birth and growth of a new religion from the midst of the Jewish people, the religion based on Jesus, the Jew from Nazareth, the teachers of the Talmud felt the need to reemphasize the uniqueness and One-ness of the God of Israel. They regarded the doctrine of the Trinity as inimical to monotheism and to the words of the Torah that "the Lord alone is our God." They were therefore involved in damage control insofar as agents of God were concerned

—and that, of course, included the entire angelic host. Even the Archangel Gabriel in the Abraham versus Nimrod story is held back from heroics. God alone would save Abraham.

Cutting angels down to size was one of the important tasks the Rabbis of the Talmud set for themselves. They interpreted Exodus 20:20—"With Me, therefore, you shall not make any gods of silver, nor shall you make for yourselves any gods of gold"—as meaning: "Do not make images of any sort of angels lest they be equated with Me." When Moses was taking down the words of the Torah as dictated to him by God he bridled at the sentence: "And God said, 'Let us make man in our image, in our likeness'" (Genesis 1:26). Moses protested: "God are you not handing heretics an argument on a silver platter?" He meant, Are you not making it possible for some to argue that in these words is proof that a man can be made to be God? God answered: "Write as I dictate, Moses. Those who choose to misinterpret, well, then, let them." On the same theme of the creation of man, a Talmudic Rabbi states that, seeing the majestic figure of Adam, the serving angels of God were ready to kneel before him and to declare: "Holy, holy, holy is the Lord of Hosts." God stayed both their knees and their voices in order to prevent a horrendous angelic blunder. So strongly did one Talmudic sage feel about the need to downgrade angels that he said: "Every single day God creates a new host of angels who, having sung His praises, vanish from the scene."

Perhaps nowhere in the Talmud is the downplaying of angels more forcefully expressed than in the order of the Seder service for the Passover holiday, which was edited under the guidance of Rabbi Gamaliel the Second, in the early decades of the second century. The verse from Deuteronomy (26:8) is first cited:

> And the Lord brought us out of Egypt with a mighty hand, with an outstretched arm, with great awe and with signs and wonders.

The comment is then made:

> And the Lord brought us out from Egypt—not by an angel, not by a seraph (fiery angel), and not by a messenger, but the Holy One, praised be He, Himself, as is implied in the verse, "I will pass through the land of Egypt that night, and I will smite all the first-born in the land of Egypt, both man and beast; and I will execute judgments against the gods of Egypt. I am the Lord." (Exodus 12:12) "I will pass through the land of Egypt": I and not an angel; "and I will smite all the first-born in the land of Egypt": I and not a seraph; "and I will execute judgment against the gods of Egypt": I and not a messenger; "I am the Lord", I and not another.
>
> (PASSOVER HAGGADAH)

The Rabbis of the Talmud devoted much effort to placing angels in their proper perspective. Primarily, this meant that to the extent that angels act at all they do so at God's behest. They are not even deputies. They are personifications of the divine will. In some Talmudic passages it seems clear that angels are used by the Rabbis as metaphors for the expression of human ideas that, if articulated by humans, might seem sacrilegious. Thus the Talmud relates that before the final decision to create man, God consulted with His inner angelic circle on the advisability of the proposed action. That inner circle consisted of the Angels of Truth, Justice, Peace, and Charity. The Angel of Truth advised against the creation of man because he foresaw that, taken in all, mankind would be chronically addicted to the violation of truth. The Angel of Justice was in favor of the idea because he foresaw that man would always be given to writing mounds upon mounds of laws. The Angel of Peace was strongly opposed to the creation of man because he saw that man's combative nature would make war a perennial fact of his existence. The Angel of Charity was enthusiastic about the great capacity man would have to bestow acts of philanthropy upon his fellows. The angelic jury was a hung one. So God took action by casting the Angel of Truth out of heaven and down to earth, thereby leaving a majority of one in favor of man's creation.

In relating this bit of allegory, the Rabbis gave a picturesque expression to several important ideas. First, there is no question of power-sharing so far as God is concerned. If there is an imaginary tale of consulting with angels it is really for the purpose of elucidating ideas germane to man's nature and destiny. Truth and peace should be the ultimate human goals, in the view of the Rabbis. Neither can be fully realized without the other. Moreover, in the absence of truth, justice is perverted and prostituted. While charity is always redemptive, it is largely necessitated by human distress and want. In a truly just world, the need for charity is sharply reduced. Finally, the seemingly unjust method used by God to settle the issue is really the major point the Rabbis were making. Truth must be thrust out of heaven toward earth. It is the one commodity most needed by the human species if it is to see itself in a light clear enough to dissipate a darkness of its own making.

## Argumentative Angels

Angels in the Talmud are frequently found in argument with God. Of course it is the Rabbis themselves who would have liked to engage in such argument in their quest to understand better the ways of the Creator, especially when they were baffled by them. Thus, as Rabbi Akiba, the shining light of his age, was being tortured to death by the Romans for the crime of teaching Torah to his disciples, the ministering angels cried out in dismay: "Is this how you, O Lord, reward those who teach your sacred law?" The divine response was immediate: "Akiba is headed for life eternal" (Talmud Berachot, 61b). The very Torah that Rabbi Akiba studied and taught all of his life was a matter of contention between God and His angelic court. How could You give so precious a treasure to sinful mortals? the angels demanded of God. Why, You created the Torah even before You created the universe, even as You chose to create us before You created man! The noble precepts of Your law will be defiled by the mortals on earth below. To which the Rabbis have God responding: What need does either heaven or its angels have for the guidance of Torah? There is no capacity for sinfulness in heaven. There are no temptations, no base feelings, no evil inclinations in the celestial regions. Ah, but the case is different with earth and the humanity that inhabits it. On earth, greed and envy and licentiousness and frustration are ubiquitous. The human being is ever besieged by his evil inclination. It is humanity that needs the guidance of Torah.

Preaching to an angelic choir is not what God had in mind. The target of God's call was mortal man, ever and always—so the Rabbis thought and taught. For it was man who was inherently insecure of his freedom to choose between good and evil. "To be or not to be" anything was the problem of mortals, not of angels. To be and to do what is pleasing to the Almighty is a daunting challenge. "Thou shalt" and "Thou shalt not" have no meaning for ephemeral angels. Therefore, the Rabbis declared, "the Torah was not given to the ministering angels."

Living under the towering shadow of disastrous exile and subjugation, the Rabbis sought to bring solace to the Jewish people through the repeated teaching that the gates of penitence are never closed, not even to the worst of sinners. Manasseh, King of Judah (about 600 B.C.E.), is described in 2 Kings, chapter 21, as the most evil of all monarchs. He instituted brazen idol worship into the Holy Temple. He sacrificed his own son to the god Moloch. He put so many innocent people to death "that he filled Jerusalem with blood from end to end." Lamentably, his bloody reign lasted fifty-five years. Manasseh, then, is a worst-case scenario in the domain of sin. Yet even the likes of Manasseh can achieve divine forgiveness if they are truly remorseful and penitent. And not even angels can stand in their way.

God had tolerated Manasseh's evildoings for twenty-two years in the hope that he would repent, as is related in the Talmud. He did not repent. So the Assyrians invaded Manasseh's kingdom of Judah, placed the king in chains of iron, and threw him into a fiery cauldron. It was then that Manasseh finally cried out to God for forgiveness and salvation. The angels attempted to block his prayers from ascending to the divine throne. They were outraged at the very idea that so late in the game so evil a man would have the audacity to address the God he had so long rejected in favor of idols of silver and gold. God overruled His angels, saying: "If I did not accept the penance of this man I should be closing the door in the face of all repentant sinners." And in the end Manasseh's genuine return to God was rewarded by his acceptance into God's grace.

A polar opposite to Manasseh was a saintly second-century Rabbi who lived in Rome, the capital city of an idolatrous empire. His purity of soul and total abstinence from sin of any kind became the stuff of rabbinic legends. But no angel, he, too, was vulnerable to temptation:

One day Rabbi Matya ben Harash was sitting in the academy, occupied with the study of Torah. His visage became as radiant as the sun and his countenance resembled that of the ministering angels . . . Satan happened at the time to pass him and (at the sight of Matya's radiant visage) was envious of him. "Is it possible," Satan wondered, "that there exists such a human who has not sinned?" He questioned God: "How do you perceive this man?" God replied: "He is perfectly righteous." Said Satan: "Grant me permission and I will pervert him." "You will fail," God said, "nevertheless, go ahead and try." Satan then appeared to Matya in the shape of the most beautiful woman to have been seen since the days of Na'amah, sister of Tubal-Cain (who had caught the eye and had seduced a leader of the Fallen Angels of yore). As soon as Matya beheld her he turned his back away. The tempting beauty came around to face him. He turned to his right. She was there. He turned left. She was still there. He could not escape the sight of her. He said: "I am fearful lest I shall be overcome by the evil inclination." He called out to one of his pupils: "Bring me fire and nails." He did so. Rabbi Matya thrust the glowing nails into his eyes, blinding himself. When Satan saw what Matya did he was seized with violent trembling and fell backwards. At that moment God summoned Raphael, the healing angel, and commanded him to restore Matya's sight. So Raphael appeared to him saying: "I am Raphael sent by the Holy One, blessed be He, to cure your blindness." Matya said: "Leave me. What was, was." Raphael reported back to God. God said: "Go back to Matya with my promise that the evil inclination will never again govern him." Thereupon, Matya permitted Raphael to heal him.[3]

Satan and the Evil Inclination *(Yetzer ha-Ra)* were frequently interchangeable in Talmudic and post-Talmudic Jewish literature. The words of God to disconsolate Cain, murderer of his brother, were always in the rabbinic mind:

> "Why are you distressed
> And why is your face fallen
> Surely, if you do right,
> There is uplift.
> But if you do not do right
> Sin crouches at the door;
> Its urge is toward you,
> Yet you can be its master!"
> (GENESIS 4:6,7)

Matya mastered the Evil Inclination. The Rabbis rejected any notion of divine dualism; that is, that there exists a god of good and light in opposition to a god of evil and darkness. The Rabbis of the Talmud strove mightily to obliterate the dualistic tendencies of the Pseudepigrapha and of the Dead Sea Scroll people. Instead, they elaborated on the dualism of the human being, the endless battle within himself between the impulse to do good and the impulse toward evil. Satan is a force *within* each of us, is really what the Matya legend is saying. We cannot get away from him because he is a part of us. We can, however, overcome him by resisting his sirenlike call and heeding instead the *Yetzer-tov*, the Good Inclination, which is also an integral part of ourselves.

In a remarkable Talmudic legend (Ketubot 77b), a battle unfolds between the saintly third-century teacher Rabbi Joshua ben Levi and no less of an adversary than the Angel of Death himself. The Rabbi emerges victorious.

One day as Rabbi Joshua was immersed in study, the shadow of the Angel of Death fell across his book. In response to the Rabbi's question as to what he was doing there, the Angel of Death announced that the Rabbi's time on earth was near expiration. Unruffled, Rabbi Joshua asked if he might be helped by the Angel of Death to scout out the place assigned to him in paradise before death actually brought him there. He caught the Angel in one of his rare good moods and was flown by him to paradise after further persuading the Angel of Death to give him his sword as assurance that death would not strike before Joshua's mission was accomplished. On the top of the wall protecting it, Rabbi Joshua looked into paradise and, sword in hand, leaped live into it. All of the angels protested the unprecedented invasion of paradise by a human still living. God hushed the angels with the firm decision that Rabbi Joshua would have his seat there. But God ordered Rabbi Joshua to return the sword to its owner, since the work of the Angel of Death is a necessity for the survival of the earth.

To overcome violence, to do away with the sword, is to see the face of God—*and live*. That is the point of the legend. Surely humanity cannot avoid death as part of the natural order. But it can be rid of the sword of violence if it is to survive collectively. Man cannot achieve the immortal status of angels but, in the words of Rabbi Akiba, "The Holy One, Blessed be He, offered him two paths: the path of life and the path of death. (Thus far) he has chosen death."

## Walking with the Right Angels

The path of life leads to God. The path of death is away from God. Said Rabbi Yochanan, the great Palestinian master of the third century: "Only angels of peace and compassion stand near The Holy One, Blessed be He. But the angels of fury are distant from His presence" (Midrash Tanhuma). The ministering angels are designated as *haverim* ("companions") because they are free of malice, hatred, envy, and competitiveness (Bar Kappara, in *Canticles Rabba*).

The path of life means walking with such angels, making *them* our companions. "If you find that a righteous man is about to start on a journey to a certain destination and you need to get there yourself, move your trip up by as much as three days or delay it by as much as three days, so that you can join him. For the ministering angels accompany him as is written (Psalms 91:11): 'For He will command His angels to guard you wherever you go.' But if you find that an evil man is about to start on a journey to the same destination you seek, advance or delay your trip by as many as three days in order to avoid his companionship, for the agents of Satan will be his company" (Tosefta Sabbath 17).

The company of both a good and a bad angel is symbolically part of any man's trip. A well-known teaching of Rabbi Yose ben Yehuda (who wrote at the end of the second century) is that "two angels accompany every man from synagogue to home on the eve of the Sabbath, one good and one bad. If he enters his house and finds the candles lit, the table set and his bed made, the good angel exclaims: 'May it be thus next Sabbath as well!' and the bad angel responds 'Amen' in spite of himself. If the case is otherwise (a messy household), the bad angel exclaims: 'May it be thus next Sabbath as well.' And the good angel responds 'Amen' in spite of himself" (Talmud Sabbath 119b).

The Sabbath is the central pillar in the house of Judaism. The second chapter of Genesis explains why:

> The heaven and the earth were finished, and all their array. On the seventh day God finished the work which He had been doing and He ceased on the seventh day from all the

*Abraham Entertains*
*Three Angels*

work which He had done. And God blessed the seventh day and declared it holy, because on it God ceased from all the work of creation which He had done.

The fourth of the Ten Commandments ordains:

Remember the Sabbath day to keep it holy. Six days you shall labor and do all your work but the seventh day is a sabbath of the Lord your God . . . For in six days the Lord made heaven and earth and sea, and all that is in them, and He rested on the seventh day; therefore the Lord blessed the Sabbath day and hallowed it.

(EXODUS 20:8–11)

The Sabbath is the bridge between God and man. It is a quintessential symbol of that measure of spirituality in human that is contained in the profound biblical statement that God created man in His image. God's angels in the above-cited passage accompany a Jew from his synagogue to his home to ascertain the kind of Sabbath spirit to be found in that home. It is in consciousness of this that a Jew begins the Sabbath eve meal with a welcoming hymn to his accompanying angels. "Shalom Aleichem" is its title. Its simple words are "Welcome and peace to you, angels of peace. Bless me with peace, you angels of peace—peace as the gift of the King who is the King of Kings, the Holy One, blessed be He."

The scholars of the Talmud, in addition to personifying

good and bad angels, brought them closer to humankind. So not only do they underscore God's One-ness by distancing Him from the angels, they also literally bring the angel down to earth.

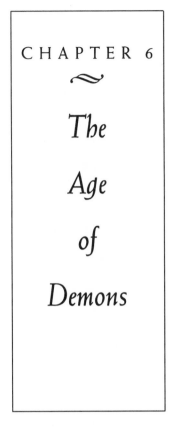

CHAPTER 6

~

*The*

*Age*

*of*

*Demons*

## What Are Demons?

~ ~ ~ ~ ~ ~ ~ ~ ~ ~ ~ ~ ~ ~ ~ ~ ~ ~ ~ ~ ~ ~ ~

Demons (*shedim* in Hebrew) make their appearance in the Hebrew Bible. "They sacrificed to demons/no-gods" (Deuteronomy 32:18) and "their own sons and daughters they sacrificed to demons" (Psalms 106:37) are two examples. That demons were not to be seen as independent powers in rebellion against God was made clear in several passages from the Talmud and Midrash. According to one passage, as God approached the end of the six days of His Creation, He was engaged in the making of souls, but He stopped as the Sabbath arrived without having supplied bodies to those souls. These "disembodied" souls are the demons (Midrash Rabba on Genesis).

Another version explains the origin of demons in the cohabitation of Adam with shady female spirits during his temporary (130 years!) separation from Eve following their expulsion from the Garden of Eden. Out of Adam's extramarital sexual activity, demons by the hundreds were born, all of them bearing the shape of human beings.

Demons as mischiefmakers infiltrated folk belief and the literature based upon it during the Middle Ages, which followed the Talmudic era. Largely, such demons were seen as invading the domain of humans in an attempt to appropriate human bodies in one way or another or to oust people from their homes and the lands on which they dwelled. Demons in Jewish folklore are associated with the satanic realm, but from time to time one discerns a certain lightness of touch, a kind of playfulness about them. Demons were brash and outspoken, like their putative king, the demon Asmodeus. In the Book of Delight, written about 1200 C.E. by Joseph Zabara, one demon recites his petrifying pedigree:

I am Enan, the Satan, son of Arnan the Demon, son of the Place of Death, son of Rage, son of Death's Shadow, son of Terror, son of Trembling, son of Destruction, son of Extinction, son of Evil-name, son of Mocking, son of Plague, son of Deceit, son of Injury, son of Asmodeus.

(AUTHOR'S TRANSLATION)

And after all this frightening self-identification, Enan quiets the fears of the human he is addressing and promises him that he would sustain no harm.

During the Middle Ages, this was wishful thinking as far as the Jews were concerned. The reality of their lives in both Christian and Islamic lands reflected the truth of Enan the Demon's boast. Terror, trembling, plague, and injury were their lot, caught as they were between the devil and deep-blue sea.

Demons are incomplete devils because there would seem to be a dimension of decency within them. This may be the idea of the Midrash, which says that they were incomplete, unfulfilled beings—disembodied spirits.

But like angels, good or bad, demons inhere in each of us. To dismiss the demonic as something "out of this world" is to be blind to those instincts within us that may erupt destructively at any moment, often disrupting our sanity and doing hurt to the lives of others. Awareness of demons thus described is a prerequisite to exorcising them. Their place in a book about angels good and bad is of crucial importance.

# Background and Sources

~~~~~~~~~~~~~~~~~~~~~~~~~~~~~~~~~~~~~~

Because a rather large number of sources have been used in researching this chapter, it may be helpful to list the most important of them here while placing them in their proper time setting.

The Church Fathers are the Christian theologians who, mainly during the first five centuries, established the dogmas that were to prevail in the Church. One of these dogmas may be described as the demonization of the Jews. This helps explain the fate of the Jews during the Crusades of 1096 and those that followed in the twelfth century. It also provides an insight into a Jewish response of, in turn, demonizing the enemy.

*The Prayer of Rabbi Simon bar Yohai*, a twelfth-century pseudepigraphic work, is a remarkable tale of the exorcism of the archdemon Asmodeus or Asmodai. It's really a thinly veiled account of Jewish suffering at the hands of both Christianity and Islam, the religion emerging in the seventh century that by the twelfth century was in fierce competition with Christianity. The Jews were caught in the middle, as the Crusades tragically demonstrated.

The *Sefer Hasidim*, or *The Book of the Pious*, was composed during the twelfth century in Germany. Its ascetic teaching, its exalted level of ethical behavior, and its common touch have made it one of the most influential texts of the Jewish Middle Ages. Demons are to be found on almost every other page and devices for their exorcism abound.

The *Zohar* is the classic book of Kabbalah, the doctrine of Jewish mysticism, composed during the thirteenth century by the Spanish-Jewish mystic Moses de Leon. Samael and Lilith, two of the most evil of demons, make frequent appearances both in the *Zohar* and the kabbalistic literature of later centuries.

*An Account of Sabbetai Zvi* is one of our important sources for the history of the false seventeenth-century Messiah whose weird distortions of Kabbalah almost undid the Jewish world. The account contains the strange tale of Rabbi Joseph della Reina, who sought to liberate the Jewish world from the clutches of Samael. His attempt ended in abysmal failure.

## Demons and History

Early in the fourth century, Christianity emerged as the state religion of the Roman Empire. Within a relatively short span of time, it spread throughout Europe, as well as to parts of Asia Minor and North Africa. Allied with the temporal powers, Christianity's posture toward Jews and Judaism was hostile. The Church Fathers, from Tertullian to Saint Augustine, had been involved in several centuries of anti-Jewish teaching. The notion of the Jews as Christ-killers, a theme originating in the New Testament, was reinforced. The idea that the Jew was either blind to or defiant of the alleged textproofs in his own Bible (the Old Testament) as to the divinity of Jesus appears with tedious consistency in the anti-Jewish polemics of the Christian theologians. The belief that Jews are condemned to be homeless wanderers on the face of the earth until they come to see the error of their ways formed the basis for anti-Jewish legislation barring them from the ownership of land and from engaging in most of the economic activities of society. From the laws of Justinian's great code in the sixth century to the legislation of the Fourth Lateran Council called by Pope Innocent III in 1215, harsh discrimination against the Jews was the norm during the Dark and Middle Ages of European history. In a word, Christianity *demonized* the Jew.

Early in the seventh century, Muhammad appeared on the world stage with dramatic flare and enormous effect. Out of the Arabian Peninsula streamed well-organized armies of the new religion of Islam, which, in a mere century, conquered huge chunks of territory in Asia, Africa, and Europe. Indeed, most of Spain and Portugal fell under the dominion of Islam, whose invading forces were finally stopped at Tours in southern France in 731.

The faith of Islam now vied with Christianity for both temporal and spiritual dominion, especially in the Mediterranean basin. The Jews fared better under Islam than they did under Christianity, although they were denied equality with the faithful and were saddled with a number of serious discriminatory regulations. In Palestine, their ancestral homeland, a small but significant community of Jews eked out a meager livelihood while assiduously cultivating their study of Torah and a life of intense piety. On the whole the relationship of the Jews with their Arab overlords was quite tolerable. To Christianity, on the other hand, the Arab occupation of the Holy Land and most especially their control over the Holy Sepulcher in Jerusalem was a bitter pill to swallow.

IN 1095, POPE Urban II called for a Crusade of Christians for the purpose of liberating Jerusalem from the control of the infidel Muslims. A ragtag army of drifters, outlaws, and debt-laden peasants joined the banners of knights and rabble-rousing monks in the march on Jerusalem. Their journey began on a southerly route along the Rhine River. The Jewish communities of Cologne, Spires, Worms, and Mayence were besieged by the crusading mobs and given the choice of baptism or the sword. The overwhelming majority of the Jews opted for death. Thousands were slaughtered or committed suicide. The Rhine, like the Nile in the days of Pharaoh, turned a bloody red.

On to Jerusalem marched the crusaders, who overcame Arab opposition in a military action that sent thousands to their death—including virtually every Jewish man, woman, and child. The so-called Latin Kingdom established Christian hegemony over the Holy Land (in 1099) that lasted until the great Kurdish general Saladin defeated the armies of Christendom during the Third Crusade, toward the end of the twelfth century (1187).

The violence of Christendom was matched by that of Islam during the twelfth century. A fanatic Islamic sect, the Almohades, founded and led by Ibn Tumart, made itself master of the Muslim possessions, both north and south of the Straits of Gibraltar. The Almohades conquered Morocco in 1146. The Jews there were given the choice of conversion to Islam or leaving the country. Many did in fact convert, while many others went to their death as martyrs to their faith. By 1149 all of southern Spain—Andalusia—had fallen to the Almohades. Jewish suffering was intense. Major academies of Jewish learning were forced to close their doors. Many Jews left Spain, including a thirteen-year-old boy who was to become the greatest Jewish teacher of his, and, perhaps, any other time. His name was Moses Maimonides.

## Enter Asmodeus, King of the Demons

Caught between the hammer and the rock—Christianity and Islam—the Jews of the twelfth century reverted to the sort of apocalyptic mood that had been spawned by the disasters of their ancestors during the Hellenistic and Roman eras. The spirit of rebellion was personified in the Persian Jew David Alroy, who marshaled a Jewish army to help Saladin in his battle against the Latin Kingdom. Alroy was real enough, but his career has become enveloped by the haze of myth (Disraeli, Prime Minister of Great Britain during the Victorian period, wrote a novel about him). An apocalyptic work in Hebrew titled *The Prayer of Rabbi Simon bar Yohai* was written during this period. Based upon a Talmudic statement (Meilah 17a,b) that during the Hadrianic persecutions Rabbi Simon was dispatched to Rome to plead for a mitigation of anti-Jewish laws, the work transfers Simon's mission to the author's own time. His references to Imperial Rome really pertain to Christian authority during the twelfth century. It begins:

> These are the hidden as well as open matters revealed to Rabbi Simon:
> He had been sent from Jerusalem to Rome to see the Emperor. While aboard ship, Asmodeus, Prince of the Demons, appeared to him in a dream, saying: "Ask of me to do what you will." "Who are you?" asked Rabbi Simon. He answered: "I am Asmodeus whom the Holy One, blessed be He, sent to perform a miracle for you." He (Simon) said: "Master of the universe! To Hagar, Sarai's handmaiden, you provided an angel and to me you send the Prince of the Demons?" Said Asmodeus: "The miracle will happen in any case. Whether I am demon or angel your need will be met." Asmodeus said further: "I am now off to take posses-

sion (of the mind) of the Emperor's daughter. I will force her to scream out: 'Rabbi Simon! Rabbi Simon' repeatedly until your arrival. They will then ask of you that you pacify me so that I would depart from the body of the princess. I will respond: 'I will not leave before everything Rabbi Simon asks for will be granted!' " Asmodeus then proceeded to the Emperor's palace and entered into the Emperor's daughter. She then began to smash everything in her father's palace while screaming: "Rabbi Simon! Simon ben Yohai!" A few days later the ship bearing Rabbi Simon arrived. The Emperor was informed and promptly sent for him asking: "What is it you came for?" He said: "The Jews of Jerusalem have sent you a gift (through me)." He said: "I want nothing from you except that you exorcise this demon who has possessed my daughter, for I have no other offspring to reign after me." Rabbi Simon then declared: "Asmodeus, leave this young woman!" He responded: "I will not leave before all your requests (of the Emperor) are granted."

(AUTHOR'S TRANSLATION)

The Emperor was ultimately persuaded to rescind the severe laws, after which Asmodeus allowed himself to be exorcised and Rabbi Simon returned to Jerusalem with letters from the Emperor restoring the Jews' right to follow their own religious regimen.

Clearly, in light of the atrocities committed against eleventh- and twelfth-century Jewry by Christendom and Islam, both were deemed to be demonic nemeses of the

Jews. Jewish hope was centered in the idea that one demon could become an instrument for the undoing of the other. In *The Prayer of Rabbi Simon bar Yohai* Asmodeus says laconically: "What difference is it to you if your miraculous deliverance is by the hand of angel or of demon? The purpose will be accomplished all the same." The message is Machiavellian, to be sure, but the potency of demons in the medieval mind had become solidly entrenched. The Jews could not help but be influenced by the folk beliefs of their neighbors. Indeed, one of the classic Jewish works of the era, the twelfth-century *Sefer Hasidim*, is fairly saturated with stories about demons as well as with incantations designed to counteract their damaging business.

As to Rabbi Simon's prayer itself, it implores God to send an angel who would answer Simon's questions: "When will the Messiah, son of David, come and how will he go about the ingathering of Israel from all the places to which they have been scattered and how many wars will they have to endure after their ingathering? . . . And, by your goodness, O Lord! How long until the end of these awful things?" (Daniel 12:6).

The angel does appear and Rabbi Simon repeats: "When will the redeemer of Israel arrive?" The anonymous angel gives Simon a glimpse of the Kenites (the Christian Crusaders) and of the Kingdom of Ishamael (the Arab-Muslim armies), who are engaged in mortal combat with each other, with now one side and now the other gaining ascendancy and with the people of Israel victimized by both. A careful reading of the fortunes of battle described in this apocalyptic vision reveals the actual facts of the history of the first three Crusades (1096–1191). The grand vision ends with the arrival of the "Great Prince," the Archangel Michael, who sounds the great horn. The Messiah, son of David, then arrives in the company of Elijah, the prophet. The dispersed children of Israel are gathered into Jerusalem and the Day of Redemption is begun.

An archdemon begins the work of salvation and an archangel completes it.

In the Rabbi Simon bar Yohai apocalypse the archdemon Asmodeus came to him uninvited. In the demonology of the post-Talmudic period, especially that of twelfth-century German Jewry, demons could be summoned by initiates in the secret lore to do their bidding. Rabbi Eliezer of Metz, a twelfth-century mystic, said that "invoking the demon to do one's will is permitted . . . for what difference is there between invoking demons or angels?" True, angels were benevolent beings, close to the presence of God and engaged in doing His will. The demons, on the other hand, possessed fearful destructive powers and weren't near the Divine Throne. Still, in an atmosphere of superstition, they were believed by ordinary folk to be useful in certain emergencies. In the *Sefer Hasidim*, attributed to the twelfth-century saint, Judah the Pious, demons are ubiquitous. Nor were they an invention of the Middle Ages. They were already found in the Talmud and Midrash, deemed "spirits of uncleanness" to be shunned as obstacles in the pursuit of the religious life.

As the Middle Ages advanced, the influence of the Christian environment affected the Jewish folk attitude toward demons. Still considered evil, demons could be exploited for good purposes. And ultimately, the demons were created by God and were therefore subject to His will: No "anti-God" can exist. It is true enough that the Pseudepigrapha, the Dead Sea Scrolls, and especially the Kabbalah evince some dualistic tendencies. But these writings are exceptional to the body of Jewish literature. And in the end, even these books came out on the side of unqualified monotheism, the absolute sovereignty of the One God.

Disembodied as demons were, they roamed the earth seeking embodiment in unsuspecting humans, especially at night and in deserted places. During the age of demons, to walk alone in the night was considered an invitation to disaster.

There was frequent rivalry, even litigation, between demons and humans. In his fascinating book *Jewish Magic and Superstition* (Jewish Publication Society, Phil., 1939), Joshua Trachtenberg writes about Jews who made their homes in an area that had already been staked out by demons somewhere in Hungary during the seventeenth century. Immediately, many of the Jews began to die at a rapid rate. Neither prayer nor fasting stemmed the tide of death, but a chance encounter by the head of the community with the master of the demons (who rode a lion, using a snake for his bridle) revealed that the community was occupying demonic turf. So the Jews moved away and the plague of death ceased.[1]

## Solomon and Asmodeus

~ ~ ~ ~ ~ ~ ~ ~ ~ ~ ~ ~ ~ ~ ~ ~ ~ ~ ~ ~ ~

Jewish lore relates that when King David was at death's door, he called in his son and successor, Solomon, for their final parting. Solomon was young, untested, and filled with unease about the crown that would soon be his. He begged his father to leave him with something that might be of help in times of crisis. His father gave him a jewel box that contained a coin. "When you are in dire straits," David said, "open this box and look at the face of the coin. When you are at the pinnacle of well-being, open it again and turn it over. Then look at the obverse side. God be with you, my son." And he died.

Years passed and Solomon found himself beset with severe problems. Mutiny was brewing in the ranks of his chief officers. The many women he married were pulling him in conflicting directions, ever setting up altars to the foreign gods they had been wont to worship. The huge economic and logistical burden of building the very first Temple for the God of Israel was close to overwhelming. Solomon's spirits were low; his soul was much aggrieved. Remembering his father's advice, he opened the jewel box and read the Hebrew words on the face of the coin: *Gam zeh ya'avor* ("This too shall pass"). He was heartened by the message and once again took control of his destiny with confidence. The obstacles were overcome. Rebellion was dissipated. A glorious Temple of God was completed, a Temple whose physical and spiritual glory overshadowed any form of alien worship in Israel. Solomon's ships sailed the high seas, bringing great prosperity to his people. From far and wide the high and the mighty made pilgrimages to pay tribute to Solomon and his riches and his wisdom. Sitting at the zenith, he forgot his father's dying words. He did not go looking for his jewel box.

Then Asmodeus, King of Demons, came knocking at his door.

Asmodeus, according to the legends of the Midrash, had been brought in chains to King Solomon because Asmodeus was privy to the whereabouts of the *shamir*, a magical rock-splitting stone needed to build the Temple. It took some very clever feats by Solomon's emissary, Benaiah, before he could capture the formidable Asmodeus. But it was the magic ring in Solomon's possession that enabled him to keep Asmodeus under subjugation. To have such power over the King of Demons was still another accomplishment that swelled Solomon's pride, even his sense of invincibility.

*The Age of Demons* ~ 163

One day the King told Asmodeus that he did not understand wherein the greatness of the demons lay, if their king could be kept in bonds by a mortal. Asmodeus replied that if Solomon would remove his chains and lend him the magic ring, he would prove his own powers. Solomon agreed. The demon stood before him with one wing touching heaven and the other reaching to the earth. Snatching up Solomon, who had parted with his protecting ring, he flung him four hundred parasangs away from Jerusalem, and then palmed himself off as the king.[2]

For three humiliating years Solomon wandered about the land of Israel, sustaining himself by begging from door to door. Over and over he exclaimed: "I am Solomon, King of Jerusalem!" He was met by derision and raucous laughter. "The wisest of men" was now thought a raving lunatic. It was a chastisement that opened his ears to a dying voice from the past. He remembered his coin and its legend: "This too shall pass." And it did. Solomon died in his royal chamber.

Solomon's arrogance had been purged by humiliation. He was fortunate to have met an Asmodeus who, by cutting him down to size, restored his spiritual stature.

∾ ∾ ∾

# Lilith

〜〜〜〜〜〜〜〜〜〜〜〜〜〜〜〜〜〜〜〜〜〜〜〜

Lilith, queen of distaff demons, looms large among Jewish folk of the Middle Ages. The name appears only once in the Hebrew Bible. Speaking of the ultimate decimation of Israel's enemy Edom, the prophet Isaiah says that in its desolate lands

> Wildcats shall meet hyenas,
> Goat-demons shall greet each other;
> There too the Lilith shall repose
> And find herself a resting place.
> (ISAIAH 34:14)

In the Talmud, Lilith is mentioned several times. She is described as lush with hair (Erubin 100b). A woman may sometimes give birth to a child in the shape of Lilith (Nidah 24b), which the great explicator of the Talmud, Rashi (1040–1104), defines as a female demon who has the face of a human but also wings. We learn that a man sleeping alone in a house is in jeopardy of being grabbed by Lilith (Sabbath 151b). The third-century *Testament of Solomon*, a book of the Pseudepigrapha, tells of a female demon known by tens of thousands of names who preys upon women in childbirth with the intent of strangling the newborn babies. But in the obscure tenth-century work *The*

*Alphabet of Ben Sira*, composed either in Persia or Arabia, a new and full account of the mysterious Lilith unfolds. As Bernard Bamberger, in his book *Fallen Angels*, tells it:

> When God perceived that it was not good for man to be alone, He first created a mate for Adam out of the dust of the earth. But the two did not get on at all, for Lilith had no feminine submissiveness about her, since her origin was identical with Adam's. She soon left him and, by pronouncing the Ineffable Name (of God), flew far away. Adam complained to God, Who dispatched three angels to force her to return. They found her among the billows of the Red Sea and threatened to drown her, especially when she declared her intention of molesting infants during the early days of their lives. But finally they let her go on this condition: if children were protected by an amulet bearing the names or pictures of the three angels she would do them no harm.[3]

Lilith was a mortal enemy of Eve and her female descendants. She was furious with the woman who supplanted her in Adam's bed and even more furious with feminine submissiveness to the masculine arrogation of superiority.

Lilith also refused to lie beneath Adam during the sexual act, deeming herself equal to him in both origin and status. The names of the angels sent to bring her back to Adam are given as Senoy, Sansenoy, and Semangelof. These names are actually found on amulets designed to protect pregnant women and newborn babies from the deadly hands of

Lilith. The earliest forms of these amulets were found in Montgomery's *Aramaic Incantation Texts from Nippur*. *The Alphabet of Ben Sira* contains the first Hebrew version of such an amulet, which includes the names of the three angels who overcame Lilith, as well as their form, wings, hands, and legs. Such amulets were printed even as late as the tenth century. Jews of the Orient prepared amulets depicting Lilith herself, bound in chains. Some amulets, Gershom Scholem writes, "include the story of the Prophet Elijah meeting Lilith on her way to the house of a woman in childbirth 'to give her the sleep of death, to take her son and drink his blood, to suck the marrow of his bones and to eat his flesh.' Elijah excommunicated her, whereupon she undertook not to harm women in childbirth whenever she saw or heard her names."[4]

It was not only women but men as well who were in need of protection from the tentacles of Lilith. Lilith and her hosts of female demons were ever on the prowl for male semen, which they needed for their own impregnation and procreation. They would slip into bed with a man alone in his room, and while he was asleep, stimulate him sexually and cause nocturnal emissions. Supposedly, the demon population was propagated from these emissions.

The offspring of Lilith herself were often fathered by men with whom she illicitly copulated at night. Lilith's children were all demons. Medieval Jewish folk believed that a man's own demonic children made claims on his inheritance and that their human half brothers should therefore recite the Ninety-first Psalm at the father's funeral to protect themselves, especially emphasizing the words "No harm will befall you, no disease will touch your tent. For He will order His angels to guard you wherever you go . . . lest you stumble on a rock."

The legend of Lilith became rather widespread in the Western world after having been first introduced to Christians by Johannes Buxdorf in the seventeenth century. Goethe made use of Lilith in his masterpiece *Faust*. Robert Browning composed a lyric poem titled "Adam, Lilith and Eve." In contemporary literature, there are still hundreds more references to Lilith, notably a publication devoted to women's rightful place in our society, felicitously titled *Lilith*.

## Lilith, the Queen of Sheba?

≈ ≈ ≈ ≈ ≈ ≈ ≈ ≈ ≈ ≈ ≈ ≈ ≈ ≈ ≈ ≈ ≈ ≈ ≈ ≈ ≈

In the masterpiece of Jewish mysticism—the "bible of the Kabbalah"—the *Zohar* ("Radiance"), Lilith plays a formidable role as the wife of Samael and queen of the realm ruled by the forces of evil, the *sitra ahara* (the left side of the ten divine emanations, or the *Sefirot*, constituting the mystery of the Godhead). But most mysterious is the *Zohar*'s identification of Lilith with the Queen of Sheba. Her debut and exit are brief and impressive, as told in 1 Kings, chapter 10:

The Queen of Sheba heard of Solomon's fame because of the Name of the Lord and she came to test him with hard questions. She arrived in Jerusalem with a very large retinue, with camels bearing spices, a great quantity of gold and precious stones. When she came to Solomon, she asked him all that she had in mind. Solomon had answers for all her questions; there was nothing that the King did not know . . . When the Queen of Sheba observed all of Solomon's wisdom, and the palace he had built, the fare of his tables, the seating of his courtiers, the service and attire of his attendants, and his wine service and the procession with which he went up to the House of the Lord, she was left breathless.

She said to the King: "The report I heard in my own land about you and your wisdom was true. But I did not believe the reports until I came and saw with my own eyes that not even the half had been told me . . . How fortunate are your men and how fortunate are these, your courtiers, who are always in attendance on you and can hear your wisdom! Praised be the Lord your God, who delighted in you and set you on the throne of Israel. It is because of the Lord's everlasting love for Israel that he made you King to administer justice and righteousness."

Solomon and Sheba then exchanged gifts. "Then she and her attendants left and returned to her own land." Though the Queen's speech was certainly gracious, according to early Arab myth she is portrayed as a Jinn (half human and half demon). A medieval mystic, Joseph Angelino, insists that the riddles the Queen of Sheba put to Solomon are a repetition of the words of seduction the first Lilith used on

Adam. Gershom Scholem writes that "until recent generations the Queen of Sheba was popularly pictured as a snatcher of children and a demonic witch."

How did a nice lady like the Queen of Sheba acquire so terrible a reputation? It might have all started with the first chapter of the biblical Book of Job, in which the first calamity inflicted upon that good man was the slaying of his seven sons and three daughters by a raiding force from Sheba (Job 1:15). The Targum (the Aramaic translation of the Hebrew Bible) speaks of Lilith, the Queen of Sheba, as heading that gory operation. Then there is the somewhat ambiguous phrase in the opening verse of the biblical Queen of Sheba story: "and when the Queen of Sheba heard of the fame of Solomon *because of the name of the Lord*" (italics added). This passage might have suggested to medieval commentators that she invoked the ineffable name of God and thereby transported herself and her entire retinue instantly to Jerusalem. Had not Lilith, first wife of Adam, translated herself to remote regions by invoking the ineffable name? Finally, the Hebrew for Sheba is *Sh'va*, meaning "captivity" or "incarceration." The Queen of Sh'va might then be conceived as the malignant demon bent on incarcerating men by trapping them unaware.

≈ ≈ ≈

*The Queen of Sheba*

# Lilith Today

〜〜〜〜〜〜〜〜〜〜〜〜〜〜〜〜〜〜〜〜〜〜〜〜

Lilith may well be the other face of Eve. If Eve is motherly, respectable, subservient to her husband, and eminently proper, Lilith is sexual, uninhibited, passionate, independent, and unconventional. And as to married males with roving eyes, they are often on the lookout for a tumble with sexy Lilith, who offers them what they feel they cannot find in their "conventional" wives. May it not be that the Lilith inherent in every woman has been suppressed by male arrogance? It seems that if there are simultaneously angels and devils within each of us, there may be polar aspects in femininity: the lady Eve and the lady Lilith.

Lilith floats through more than four thousand years of legend, fable, and folklore with undiminished zest—longer than any other demon in mythological literature. The words of Dante Gabriel Rosetti, written some one hundred and fifty years ago, are still on the mark:

> Of Adam's first wife Lilith, it is told
> (The witch he loved before the gift of Eve)
> That, ere the snake's, her sweet tongue could deceive,
> And her enchanted hair was the first gold.
> And still she sits, young while the earth is old,
> And, subtly of herself contemplative,
> Draws men to watch the bright web she can weave,
> Till heart and body and life are in its hold.

Lilith has survived because, though demonized by a literature written by men, she's no demon. She is an essential aspect of a womanhood consigned to nether status by the fear and ambivalence of "manhood." Adam wanted his Eve to lie beneath him. The Lilith within Eve rebelled against that arrogance and demanded an egalitarian relationship, a challenge that men could not ignore. The method they chose for dealing with it was the banishment of Lilith to the regions of sorcery and witchcraft, to the waters of the Nile and the fires of Salem. But Lilith would not be banished, not unless humanity was to be banished with her.

## The Dybbuk

Possession of places and houses by demons didn't have to be catastrophic for those who knew enough to run away. But what if a demon possessed a living human being, such as the Emperor's daughter in the tale of Rabbi Simon bar Yohai? That was a horrifying eventuality to the medieval mind. The victim became an unwilling tool for the machinations of the spirit that possessed him, and, of course, the possessed no longer had a mind of his own. He became demented, hysterical, and often violent. He lost his own persona. He was possessed by a dybbuk.

More often than not, the dybbuk was the spirit of a dead person who had either committed a terrible sin during his lifetime, a sin that had to find its atonement through the life of another person, or who had been terribly sinned against while he was alive and was seeking to right that wrong through possessing the body of the perpetrator. An example of the first case is, indeed, the first appearance of a dybbuk in Jewish literature, included in the *Ma'aseh Book* (1602). An example of the second case is S. An-Sky's classic drama *The Dybbuk*, composed some seventy years ago and subsequently made into a marvelous Yiddish film. In An-Sky's story, an agreement is reached and sworn to by two friends that their infant children when grown would marry one another. The oath is violated when the girl's father eventually marries her off to someone else. The promised groom, in love with his promised bride, as she is with him, has died of heartbreak. At her wedding his spirit enters the body of his beloved and she plunges into insanity. The drama ends with the proverbial successful operation and dead patient. The possessing demon is exorcised by a holy Rabbi but the lady falls dead.

≈ ≈ ≈

# Demons and the Kabbalah

〰〰〰〰〰〰〰〰〰〰〰〰〰〰〰〰〰

We have already encountered Samael. He receives dishonorable mention many times in the literature of Talmud and Midrash, where he is frequently identified with the Serpent, with Satan, and with the Angel of Death. The Midrash describes him as the very incarnation of evil and the celestial patron of the corrupt Roman Empire. He was involved in the seduction of Adam and Eve. He was a leader of the Fallen Angels, whose story is so cryptically told in Genesis, chapter 6. He brought accusations against the Children of Israel designed to prevent their Exodus from Egyptian bondage. He danced with joy upon the death of Moses. He entered the soul of Manasseh, King of Judah, causing the unspeakable evil acts of that sovereign. He was, in sum, the unchallenged prince of the demons.

No wonder that Jewish mysticism, the Kabbalah, arrived at the belief that Samael was the husband of Lilith. They were a perfect match. No wonder, either, that in the Kabbalah's architectonic picture of good versus evil—*sitra di yemina* (the right side of the divine emanations) versus *sitra ahara* (the "other," or the left side), Samael is the dominant force of the latter. To overcome Samael and his formidable demonic host was one of the major aims of the practitioners of the Kabbalah, especially as taught by Rabbi Isaac Luria (1534–1572) and his school in the Galilean town of Safed during the sixteenth century.

The late Gershom Scholem was the master scholar of the history and the doctrines of Jewish mysticism known as the Kabbalah. No serious study of Judaism can now be undertaken without reference to the rich opus Scholem has left behind. Nor can much space be devoted within the confines of our theme in this book to elaboration on the teachings of the Kabbalah. A few facts and ideas are, however, necessary as background to what will immediately follow.

Alongside the regnant "official" teaching of the Rabbis there had existed from the end of the Jewish biblical era (about 200 B.C.E.) a mystic strand in the tradition, traces of which are found in the Talmud itself. That strand was concerned with ultimate questions about God and His Creation, and explored these questions in the texts of the opening chapters of Genesis, where the Creation story is told, and the first chapter of Ezekiel, which describes the prophet's vision of the Lord's chariot. The Genesis chapters are called *Ma'asei Bereshith*, or "Matters Concerning Creation." The Ezekiel chapter is designated *Ma'asei Merkava*, or "Matters Concerning the Chariot," and speculates about the nature of God.

The Rabbis of the Talmudic period vigorously discouraged popular speculation on either of these matters because they regarded it as dangerous for the average Jew (or even the average Rabbi) to delve into deep mysteries that only the most spiritually gifted might venture to inspect. Study of divine mysteries was, to the mind of the Rabbis, an attempt to force open the gates of paradise, from which

Adam and his progeny had been expelled. It was fraught with mortal danger and could lead to apostasy, insanity, or death.

Toward the end of the thirteenth century, Moses de Leon, a Spanish mystic, produced a manuscript, the *Zohar* (or *The Book of Radiance*), which he claimed was the work of the second-century Rabbi Simon bar Yohai.

Zoharic Kabbalah undertook to bridge the huge chasm between God, the unknowable and transcendent, and the material cosmos He created. Most especially the Kabbalah's teaching is designed to bring the divine presence—the *Shekhinah*—into closer contact with human beings. The Torah contains within it not only the overt prescriptions for the behavior of Jews (the *mitzvot*) but also the covert meaning that underlies each of the *mitzvot* and the *kavanah* (intent) with which they are to be performed. This is esoteric knowledge, the revelation of which is the privilege of an elite coterie of initiates.

Less than a hundred years after the Kabbalah was written, the situation of the Jews in Spain began to deteriorate rapidly with the terrible massacres of Seville in 1391. A Jewish community of a thousand years' standing was suddenly subjected to relentless persecutions that climaxed with the inauguration in 1482 of the Spanish Inquisition, culminating ten years later with the expulsion of the Jews from Spain. Some 150,000 refugees, stunned, bewildered, and pathetic, sought homes wherever they could: They went to Holland, Italy, Turkey. Some eventually even found their way to the newly discovered Americas. And some returned to the ancestral homeland, Eretz Yisrael.

It was in the tiny Galilean town of Safed that a circle of mystics gathered during the middle of the sixteenth century under the inspiration of Rabbi Isaac Luria, whose own interpretation of Kabbalah exerted enormous influence upon Jewish history and Jewish theology in the centuries to follow. Lurianic Kabbalah, as it came to be called, added some crucial elements to the accepted mystical thought. In a shattered Jewish world fresh from the prodigious trauma of the Spanish expulsion and in quest of answers to the questions "Why" and, of course, "What is going to be?" Luria offered a remarkable paradigm. A world that was good and whole had been shattered by the sin of primordial man, who was also a configuration of God Himself, having been created in His image. God's original design thus became fragmented. The shards *(Kelippot)* are the evil forces all about us that are sustained by the divine sparks *(Nitzot-zot)* that cling to them. The task of the practicing Jew is to collect the divine sparks by removing them from the *Kelippot*. Once separated, the *Kelippot* are left lifeless and their potential for evil is eliminated. When all the sparks have been gathered, the goodness and wholeness of God's original cosmic design would be restored and the redemption, so long and so longingly sought, would be at hand.

Every mitzvah properly understood and performed is an act of *Tikkun*, of repair. Man becomes actively involved in the reconstitution of the Creation. The battle against

Samael and his cohorts must be relentless. Evil in the form of the *Kelippot* and the demons must be hounded and extirpated by depriving it of the source of all life—God, the Creator.

Lurianic mystics had frequent encounters with guardian angels, at least in their dreams. One of the most influential Rabbis of any age was Joseph Karo (1488–1575) of Safed, a prodigious scholar of Jewish law (Halakah) whose *Shulhan Arukh* is *the* definitive code of laws by which observant Jews are still guided. He was also a mystic who wrote about visitations from his own *Maggid*, or celestial teacher, who often instructed him what to write and what to say. Lurianic Kabbalists were also given to summoning both angels and demons by using intricate combinations of the names of God, literally numbering in the hundreds. They did not think of this as magic (though, in effect, it was), since God Himself was the means by which they were seeking certain ends.

## Joseph della Reina and Samael

~ ~ ~ ~ ~ ~ ~ ~ ~ ~ ~ ~ ~ ~ ~ ~ ~ ~ ~ ~

The story of Joseph della Reina (in one version his name is Joseph Dolphina) is an eerie illustration of Kabbalistic incantation. A number of scholars, including Zalman Shazar, former president of the state of Israel, and Gershom Scholem, have attempted to place this story into some kind of historical context. A Yiddish version of the tale *An Account of Sabbetai Zvi* completed in 1718 was included in the memoirs of Leib ben Ozer Rosencrantz, sexton of the Ashkenazic Synagogue in Amsterdam.

The gist of the tale is as follows: A very pious man, Rabbi Joseph, living in the holy city of Hebron, was totally immersed in the study of the Kabbalah. He sought out ten soulmates who joined him in fasting and in prayer while poring over the mysteries of the *Zohar* night and day. Rabbi Joseph wept in mourning over the destruction of the Holy Temple and prayed mightily for some divine illumination. It was finally granted to him in the form of an encounter with Elijah, the prophet, who began to teach him much secret lore, including the proper combination of God's holy names. Rabbi Joseph then pleaded with God to reveal to him the time of the arrival of the Messiah and the ingathering of the scattered Jewish people. Elijah reprimanded him for seeking an answer that had not been given even to the holiest and most worthy. But Rabbi Joseph became more importunate than ever, and besought Elijah to at least reveal to him the means by which he, Joseph, might accelerate the advent of the redemption and exterminate the impurities, the *Kelippot*, and the adversaries from the face of the earth. Elijah finally yielded, informing Rabbi Joseph that his mighty prayers had induced heaven to divulge the secret of Samael's headquarters and to instruct Joseph on how to get there and put Samael in chains. With the incantation of certain holy names, Joseph and his ten disciples would arrive at the mountains of darkness and Samael would appear to them in the shape of the blackest of hounds. Elijah supplied Joseph with a chain on which was engraved the Ineffable Name of God, and he gave him pure frankincense, whose aroma would provide Joseph and his disciples with the strength to withstand the hound's unbearably foul stench. The chain was to be cast around the hound, who had to be immediately slaughtered. Elijah solemnly warned that Joseph must not be beguiled by any of the hound's blandishments, no matter what.

Faithfully following Elijah's instructions, Joseph and his disciples soon found themselves in the mountains of darkness with the black hound. The chain was promptly cast about the creature, who immediately began to wail bitterly and to plead for mercy. He was ignored as the Kabbalists got ready to slaughter him. At the last minute the hound pleaded: "As a final wish please let me smell the pure frankincense." They dropped their guard long enough to comply. Immediately the hound jumped up and exclaimed: "Master of the Universe, your Torah forbids the worship of alien gods, yet these people have just offered me pure frankincense!" (an important element of the service of God in the Holy Temple). Thereupon the black hound broke his chains and cast each of the company into faraway places. That very year most of them either died or lost their sanity. Joseph was among the latter. He found himself in the Kingdom of France, where through his magical incantations he seduced the beautiful Queen Dolphina, who engaged in nightly sex with him. In a state of somnambulism, she was involved with Joseph in this way for two months until finally she was able to tell her husband the King about her eerie aberration. The Jewish community was then ordered to bring Rabbi Joseph to the presence of the King. At the end of his rope, Joseph committed suicide by jumping from a high cliff.

Leib Ben Ozer's account ends with the words: "The King was told that Joseph had committed suicide due to insanity. The King ordered that he be buried with great honors, for the King had heard that the departed had once been a great man and that what he had done was the result of his madness."

This tale of the supernatural was transmitted by a man who was witness to one of the greatest explosions of madness in Jewish history. A Turkish Jew, Sabbetai Zvi (1626–1676), proclaimed himself the Messiah in 1665 and came to be accepted as such by a large part of the world's Jewish population. In the end, faced with an ultimatum by the Turkish Sultan, Sabbetai converted to Islam. But so great was the spell this "Messiah" cast upon his followers that many persisted in their belief in him, even after his death in exile on a lonely Albanian island. Remnants of underground Sabbatian sects survived almost into the twentieth century.

The tale of Rabbi Joseph della Reina and his confrontation with Samael is of Sabbatian provenance. The descent into madness and messianic aspirations inform the whole of it. Incantations, constantly in use by Sabbetai and his followers, are also essential to the plot. Finally, the sexual perversions of Sabbetai (of which there were many) are paralleled by the liaison of Joseph and Queen Dolphina.

The Sabbatian movement and its inglorious end may be regarded as respectively the climax and the ending of the age of demons. The aftermath of the false messiah was a sobering-up process for the Jewish masses and the genesis of a premodern era in which the demonic element began to recede and the dangers of unfettered Kabbalistic imagination were clearly perceived by responsible Jewish leadership. Mysticism was not dead, to be sure, but its demonic pathways were no longer thoroughfares in the journeys of the Jewish people. A new age was on the horizon, one in which a mighty struggle between tradition and modernity would be inaugurated. The guardian angel of the people Israel was back again at the Red Sea, where the waters were once again divided but without Moses to lead the way. Therefore, there were *two* possible sea-lanes to navigate.

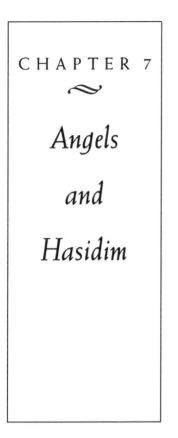

CHAPTER 7

~

*Angels*

*and*

*Hasidim*

## Hasidim in the Age of Enlightenment

~ ~ ~ ~ ~ ~ ~ ~ ~ ~ ~ ~ ~ ~ ~ ~ ~ ~ ~

The demons of folk illusion were largely dispelled by the spirit of the Age of Enlightenment—the eighteenth century. In western Europe particularly, philosophers and scientists of high repute challenged much of the wisdom of the past, including the hallowed tenets of religion. God Himself was the target of doubts as skepticism in all matters became the mode among the well educated. Such an environment was inhospitable to demons, hobgoblins, and shades.

Naturally, the Jewish world was affected by the winds of change, and a movement called Haskalah (*Haskalah* is Hebrew for "enlightenment") sprang up in the Jewish communities of western Europe. Moses Mendelssohn, the father of the Haskalah, was born in Germany in 1729. The Haskalah advocated Jewish assimilation into greater society.

Meanwhile, in 1700 in Poland, Israel Ba'al Shem Tov, father of the Hasidic movement, was born. Contrary to the Haskalah, Hasidim were fiercely traditional, encouraging Jews to maintain distinctiveness from society—even in their dress and speech. It's interesting that these completely disparate movements both grew out of an atmosphere of despair that enveloped the Jews of Poland at that point in time as a result of the massacres of 1648 and 1649. The Ukrainian Cossacks had led revolts, killing more than 100,000 Jews and destroying scores of Jewish communities in the process. The physical damage, enormous as it was, was perhaps overshadowed by the psychic malaise that ensued.

The Hasidim, with their passionate belief in the nearness of the Messiah and the joyous, spirited way they prayed, sang, and celebrated God and their own togetherness, breathed life and enthusiasm into people who were once again at the abyss of despair. Despite their self-induced isolation from the rest of the world, within the Hasidic community there was tremendous warmth and closeness—fraternity inspired not only by sharing prayers but also by communal meals, shared rites of passage, and a common favorite pastime: the telling of tales about the feats of their masters, especially Ba'al Shem Tov.

To answer the big questions about God, His promises, and redemption, the Hasidic teachers were the first to use storytelling as a vehicle for spreading the good word.

Scores of compilations of tales about the *Tsadikkim* recount miraculous deeds wrought by the holy masters through their ability to invoke heaven's aid. Like Jesus in the Gospels, they exorcised demons, healed the hopelessly sick, and occasionally even raised the dead. They could experience *Kfitzat ha-derekh* (the ability to traverse immense distances in no time) almost at will. Their eyes could penetrate the souls of people so that they could both describe a person's past and foretell a person's future. They had frequent encounters with the prophet Elijah. They sometimes journeyed to heaven and back on the urgent business of bringing help to suffering Jews. Their standing with God was such that they would often successfully countermand an edict issued by the Creator Himself.

It's hard to accept that the Hasidim actually believed these tales, but to understand the phenomenon of Hasidism we must scratch beneath the surface of their far-fetched fables. They bespeak the power of faith in the face of disaster. They provide models of decency and compassion in the description of the masters, the *Tsadikkim*, who also serve as the champions of the tradition in an age of increasing religious skepticism. The optimism and elation in the tales enabled them to overcome the stark mood of the "valley of the shadow of death."

## Angels Are Created by Humans

How do angels, devils, and demons fare in Hasidic literature? To address the question it is best, I think, to invoke the Hasidic method of teaching, the tale itself.

> A thief in his old age was unable to ply his "trade" and was starving. A wealthy man, hearing of his distress, sent him food. Both the rich man and the thief died on the same day. The trial of the rich man occurred first in the Heavenly Court. He was found wanting and sentenced to Purgatory. As he was about to enter, an angel came hurrying to recall him. He was brought back to the Heavenly Court to be told that his sentence was canceled because the thief he had helped on earth had stolen the ledger of the rich man's sins.[1]

To help other humans in distress, even thieves, is to build one's credentials for the Kingdom of Heaven. *Havruta* (compassion for others) is a seminal Hasidic doctrine. Another tale illustrates this doctrine beautifully: Two Hasidim are supporting each other on the way home late one night from their Rebbe's table, where they had had a bit too much to drink. Mendel: "Yoskeh, do you love me?"—"Of course I do!"—A few moments of silence. Mendel: "Yoskeh, can you tell me what is hurting me?"—"Of course not. I am not a diviner!"—Mendel: "Then, Yoskeh, you lied when you said that you loved me!"

A recurrent Hasidic theme is that to identify with the pain of the other gives meaning to love. The Hasidim believed that angels identified the individuals they accompanied. A deed of kindness created a kind angel. A deed of cruelty created a cruel angel. In this belief, Hasidic teaching was true to the lore of the Talmudic Rabbis in that the identity of angels could be found within the character of the individual.

A man died and was brought before the Heavenly Court. His sins and good deeds were placed on the scales, and the sins outweighed the good deeds. Suddenly an angel placed a fur-coat on the scale holding the good deeds. That was enough to tilt it in the man's favor and he was accordingly sent to Paradise. He said to the angel who escorted him: "I do not understand the matter of the fur-coat." The angel responded: "One cold winter night you traveled on a sleigh and picked up a poor man on the way. You noticed that he was shivering. You took off your fur-coat and had him put it on. That fur-coat weighed more than you thought . . ."

The escorting angel in this tale was the reflection of compassion created by an act of compassion. Angels of another sort may also be created:

> A certain man in Kolomeya learned that the Ba'al Shem Tov was in town for the Sabbath. He made scornful remarks to his wife at the evening meal for the Sabbath regarding the work of the Ba'al Shem. Next morning he ran into the Ba'al Shem who, much to his surprise asked: "Is it right for a good Jew to speak ill of a fellow Jew, and on the Holy Sabbath at that?" The man retorted: "Do angels, then, engage in carrying tales abroad from the privacy of a man's home?" "Yes, indeed," answered the Ba'al Shem, "mockery and a tongue of evil create an angel whose task it is to tell one and all how and why he came to be formed."

There is ample evidence in Hasidic literature that the very function, if not the very existence, of angels stems from the deeds of man. The Rabbi of Kobrin interpreted the famous dream of Jacob's ladder such that man is the ladder standing on earth, with the top rung reaching heaven. Whether angels are going up or going down depends entirely on what man does.

≈ ≈ ≈

# Of Humans and Angels

The *Maggid* (preacher) of Kobrin was known for the beautiful melodies he set for the daily prayers. The greatest of these melodies became the precious legacy that identified his band of Hasidim wherever they traveled. It was said among them that he had heard this melody sung by the angels during their daily paeans to God. However, this was contradicted by one of his most loyal disciples, who claimed that the angels were created by the good works of the *Maggid* and it was *he* who taught *them* the melody.

Though we also create bad angels, we can always escape them by true penitence, according to the Hasidim:

> Our sages teach that a penitent may gain access to places in heaven from which even perfectly righteous people are barred. Rabbi Israel Isaac of Alexander explained this in a parable:

> A man visited the King's palace and was told that he may not open any doors marked "private." Next day he was pursued by a gang of ruffians and to evade them he darted into a room marked "private." He explained the violation as the result of his fear of being slain by the ruffians. His action was therefore excused.

"In the same way," the Rabbi concluded, "the penitent escaping the evil angels created by his sins, is allowed access to the secret chambers of heaven, entry to which is denied even to the *Tsadikkim*."

To the Hasidim, a penitent person—a *ba'al teshuvah*—stood in the very highest spiritual degree, for he had had to overcome the mountainous obstacles created by his sinfulness and the hosts of bad angels who were born of his misdeeds.

Once, Rabbi Moshe of Kobrin lifted his eyes heavenward and exclaimed: "O angel on high, it takes no special effort to be an angel in heaven. You need neither food nor drink. You do not need to bring children into the world and then struggle to see them reared properly. Just come down to earth and let's see if in obligation to all these things you will remain an angel. If you succeed in that, you may well boast of your angelic nature. But not until then."

It is easy to achieve perfect harmony in heaven because heaven is not subject to conflicts. Not so on earth, where chaos is rampant.

A man once came to the Rabbi of Lekhivitz to complain that his awareness of his failures in the service of God led him to frequent fits of melancholy. Said the Rabbi: "Let me tell you a parable from which you may derive some comfort.

"A King had a palace orchestra which performed music at his pleasure. He also had a nightingale which sang out from time to time. The King enjoyed the natural untutored melodies of the nightingale more than the studied harmonies of his orchestra.

"The King of Kings has hosts of angels who sing before him in perfect harmony, yet He prefers to hear the imperfect and oft-times discordant praise of us mortals. As long as we offer our service to the best of our ability, we need never feel disheartened at our shortcomings."

The melody—or, as the Hasidim call it, the *niggun*—was both reality and metaphor to the Hasidim. It was more often than not a song without words, and it was always charged with a deep love of God. Ultimately, all *niggunim* are addressed to the *Ribbono Shel Olam*, the Master of the Universe, sometimes through the offices of angels who were designated as *machnisei rahamim*, "the beings who bring prayers for compassion" into the presence of the divine addressee. Alternately, these good angels were described as *machnisei dim'ah*, "the beings who bring human tears" into the presence of the Creator.

≈ ≈ ≈

# The Niggun in the Air

~~~~~~~~~~~~~~~~~~~~~~~~~~~~~~~~~~~~~~~~~~~~~~~~~~~~~

A *niggun* came to play a pivotal role in my own life following the Passover holiday of 1949. My mother had
a heart attack, which was to kill her within twenty-four
hours. She was fifty-seven. Mother had always wanted to
be buried in Israel, where she was born, a sixth-generation
Sabra. My family designated me to fly from New York to
Israel to await the arrival by boat of my mother's body and
to see to the details of the burial. I was seated on an El Al
plane next to a Hasidic Jew who was engaged through
most of the trip in reciting the Book of Psalms. My heart
was weighted down with grief. From time to time I could
not hold back my sadness. The Hasid interrupted his quiet
recitation, turned toward me, and said in Yiddish: "You
are in deep pain, young man. You have lost someone, is
that not so?" "I have lost my mother, and am on my way to
Eretz Yisrael to see to her burial," I responded. After a few
moments of silence, he said: "As you can see, I'm reciting
*Tehillim* (the Psalms). I am at Psalm Twenty-seven. If you
do not regard it as inappropriate, I would like to sing you a
bit of a *niggun* for the passage, 'Though my father and
mother abandon me/the Lord will take me in/Show me
Your way, O Lord and lead me on a level path.' " I nodded
my assent. Then I heard the *niggun* of my life—soft and
plaintive, ethereal and calming, tearful and mending—all
at the same time. The Hasid hummed it several times at my

*Angels and Hasidim* ~ *193*

request and then I sang along with him. He said: "Young man, the pilot said we are thirty-two thousand feet above ground. The angels are carrying our *niggun* much higher, to the Throne of God, to where your mother's soul is now at rest."

I was at rest for the balance of the trip. My mother was buried in the family plot of the Nahalat Yitzhak Cemetery in Tel Aviv. My eulogy at her graveside was the story I am now sharing with you.

But there is a postscript. Some time later, while I was still in Israel, I read in the morning paper that Rabbi Shaul Taub, the leader of the Modzhitz Hasidim, had died. I looked at the picture of the deceased and recognized the man who bequeathed his *niggun* to me. It was the closest I have ever come to meeting an angel face-to-face.

## Prenatal Angels

When a child is still in its mother's womb, an angel teaches it all of the wisdom of the Torah, by means of which salvation is attainable and suffering is eradicated. However, just before the child is to see the light of day, another angel arrives to pat the child's mouth, causing it to forget everything it had learned. Rabbi Baruch of Medzibozh, grandson of the Ba'al Shem Tov, questioned the point of all this. One angel giveth and another taketh away? He answered his own questions, saying that the angel in charge of forgetfulness was performing a most vital function, for were it not for the fact that humans forget, they would live every minute in dread of death. Then why teach the unborn child in the first place if he is to be made to forget before he can even begin to make use of the teaching? Rabbi Baruch said that in the recesses of the child's mind the impression of the teaching remains. It then becomes the challenge of every life to bring that teaching out into the open, allowing the teaching angel to have the last word.

## "To Break Off Every Yoke"

This doctrine, that we must pay attention to the godliness within, is an all-important teaching of the Hasidic masters. The lot of suffering people was always on their agenda, and to their plight, the masters were prepared to move heaven and hell. The mandate "to break off every yoke" was especially sacred to them, as indeed it had been throughout the history of diaspora Jewry. Wars and sheer malevolence often led to the capture and ransom of Jews. *Pidyon Shevuyim*, ransoming the imprisoned, was a mitzvah of highest priority: Every Jewish community had a fund for just that purpose. The Hasidic master Moshe Leib of Sasov made that his life's work.

It is told that when Rabbi Moshe Leib of Sasov died, he said to himself: "Now I am exempt from all of the commandments. How could I now fulfill the will of the Creator, blessed be He?" Upon reflection he concluded: "Doubtless the will of the Creator, blessed be He, must be that I be punished for the innumerable sins I have committed!" He therefore ran with all his might and jumped into the hellfire. There was immediate turmoil in heaven. The angel in charge of hell received an order to stop the fires so long as the Rabbi of Sasov remained there. The angel begged the Rabbi to remove himself to Paradise, where he belonged. It disturbed the order of things that the fires of hell should cease on his account. "If that be the case," said Rabbi Moshe Leib, "I will not budge until all the suffering souls in hell come with me. My life on earth was engaged in the redemption of captives and I will not allow this large hoard to suffer captivity!"

There could be no heaven for Moshe Leib as long as the fires of hell were ablaze for others. Rabbi Bunem was asked why it was written "I am the Lord your God who took you out of the land of Egypt" instead of "I am the Lord your God who created heaven and earth?" He answered that "heaven and earth" is an abstraction, but that removing people from slavery is something anyone can understand. "God's mandate to us," he said, "is to pull suffering people from the pits in which they are confined."

≈ ≈ ≈

# Out of the Fire

~~~~~~~~~~~~~~~~~~~~~~~~~~~~~~~~~~~~~~~~~~

"God's mandate to us," said Rabbi Moshe Leib of Sasov, "is to pull suffering people from the pits in which they are confined." In Jewish history that mandate was rarely carried out. In our own century of catastrophe, too many averted their eyes from the fires that were consuming millions of human beings in the death camps of swastika-bearing demons. One and a half million Jewish children were incinerated while the world looked the other way. The Holy Church itself had set a precedent for burning people alive as far back as the French, Spanish, Portuguese, and Papal inquisitions. Thousands of spectators were on hand for the ceremonial, celebratory autos-da-fé of the Inquisition in which Marranos, Spanish Jews, were tied to stakes and burned to ashes. No one rushed into the flames of the *Gehenna* on earth to pull alleged sinners from the fire. So the Marranos dreamed of savior angels. There was "the damsel of Herrera," Ines, daughter of the cobbler Estevan, who claimed that she visited the angels in heaven from time to time and was shown by one of them a celestial chamber from which she heard the sweetest singing. The angel told Ines that the people who burned below on earth who were now in the closest proximity to the Creator Himself were making the divine music.

There were other suffering visionaries—Marranos like the young woman of Chillon in the province of Ciudad

Real—who claimed to have had similar angelic encounters. A Marrano woolcomber from Almodovar del Campo fasted several days each week and claimed that thereby he was granted a visit to the Garden of Eden, where he actually saw God, Elijah the Prophet, and the Messiah in consultation on the imminent salvation of the Jews, including all of the Marranos who remained believers. Supposedly, they would all be transported on clouds and on the wings of angels to Eretz Israel, and God would send abundant supplies of foods and goods from his heavens. The believers who had been burned would be resurrected so they could partake in the sweetness of the redemption.

An apocalyptic fervor seized the Marrano communities of Castille as a result of the well-broadcast visions of God and angels, of Elijah and the Messiah, of vindication and bliss. Many were seized with visions of Abraham and Moses in their own homes. An otherworldly light suffused their dwellings. These tragic ex-Jews who had been forced into baptism were so certain of their imminent release from inquisitorial darkness that they bought spanking-new garments for the great day that was coming.

All of this is documented in the archives of the Inquisition itself: Every one of the dreamers was apprehended and burned by the zealots of the Christian faith. And there was no Rabbi Moshe Leib of Sasov to plunge in and pluck brands from the fire.

~ ~ ~

THE *NIGGUN* OF the Rabbi of Modzhitz is always with me. It is a melody of love among the ruins, a song of life in the face of death, a leap into and out of the flames of *Gehenna*, a call out of the dark to the angel of light.

To Hasidic thought, angels were also to the right, to the left, and in front of every human being. His thoughts, his moods, and his actions could all share an angelic spirit if he would allow himself to be transported by them into the presence of the divine.

Like the very first Hasidim who survived the atrocities in Poland two centuries earlier, the Hasidim who survived the Holocaust became a powerful force in traditional Judaism both in the United States and in Israel. Today's Hasidim are still somewhat isolated from the rest of society, even from other Jews, due to their rigid beliefs and strict adherence to Jewish law and tradition. But exultant in prayer, and with hearts open to God, they remain in the company of angels.

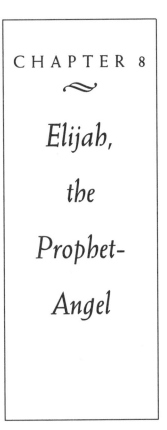

CHAPTER 8

~

*Elijah,*

*the*

*Prophet-*

*Angel*

## Elijah, the Living Legend
~ ~ ~ ~ ~ ~ ~ ~ ~ ~ ~ ~ ~ ~ ~ ~ ~ ~ ~ ~ ~

Of a sudden, Elijah the Prophet appeared to Ahab, King of Israel, and said: "As the Lord lives, the God of Israel whom I serve, there will be no dew or rain except at my bidding" (1 Kings 17:1).

We are told nothing about Elijah except that he was a Tishbite, an inhabitant of Gilead. The mysterious arrival of Elijah was surpassed only by his dramatic departure from the earthly scene. Elijah struck the waters of the river Jordan with his rolled-up mantle, causing it to part. Then he and his designated successor, Elisha, crossed the river. During the crossing:

> Elijah said to Elisha, "Tell me, what can I do for you before I am taken from you?" Elisha answered "Let a double portion of your spirit pass on to me." "You have asked a difficult thing," he said. "If you see me as I am being taken from you, this will be granted to you; if not, it will not." As they kept on walking and talking, a fiery chariot with fiery horses suddenly appeared and separated one from the other; and Elijah went up to heaven in a whirlwind. Elisha saw it, and he cried out, "Oh, father, father! Israel's chariots and horsemen!" When he could no longer see him, he grasped his garments and rent them in two.
>
> (2 KINGS 2:6–12)

A living legend while on earth, Elijah became a celestial legend in Jewish tradition, one who, like Enoch, was translated heavenward without undergoing the intermediary stage of death. Indeed, in the literature of Midrash, Elijah and Enoch are often one and the same person. Since heaven is no place for mortals, Elijah the immortal became the most active angel in all of Jewish lore, and the most beloved.

As a Jewish boy is circumcised on the eighth day of his life, a prayer is recited: "Elijah, angel of the Covenant, stand at my right hand and support me." At the Passover Seder table, a cup of wine is filled for Elijah, and the door is opened to welcome him inside. When the Rabbis of the Talmud could not resolve a point of law among themselves, they often brought the issue to a close with the statement "Let it rest, pending the arrival of Elijah." The very last words of prophecy in the Hebrew Bible read:

> Lo, I will send the Prophet Elijah to you before the coming of the awesome, fearful day of the Lord. He shall reconcile fathers with sons and sons with their fathers, so that, when I come, I do not strike the whole land with utter destruction.
>
> (MALACHI 3:23)

It is from this passage that there emerged the Jewish (and Christian) tradition of Elijah as herald and forerunner of the Messiah.

In heaven proper, Elijah is the angel who records the deeds of human beings (Talmud Kidushin 70). He is stationed at the crossroads of paradise and escorts the pious to their appointed places there. At the onset of the Sabbath he leads the denizens of hell out of its fires and returns them there when the Sabbath is out. He shuttles between heaven and earth with such frequency that the Midrash dubs him "the bird of heaven" who swoops onto the stage of earth whenever situations of crisis require his immediate intervention.

No other character in the Hebrew Bible has received as much attention as Elijah has through successive periods of Jewish writing down to the present day. To account for this, it is necessary first to examine the pertinent biblical material contained in 1 Kings, chapters 17 through 22, and 2 Kings, chapters 1 and 2.

## Elijah and Ahab

≈≈≈≈≈≈≈≈≈≈≈≈≈≈≈≈≈≈≈

Elijah's activity coincided with the reign of Ahab, King of Israel, toward the first half of the ninth century B.C.E. It had been about sixty years since the kingdom over which David and then Solomon ruled was splintered in half. The dynasty of David continued its reign from Jerusalem, where the Holy Temple had been built by Solomon. The division of the kingdom had resulted in the establishment of another capital in the city of Samaria, whose authority extended over the northern part of Eretz Israel. The seceding kingdom was variously called Ephraim—after its most powerful tribe—or simply Israel. The dynasty of David ruled over what was then called Judah, after its dominant tribe. In the main, the Kingdom of Judah included the tribes of Judah, Benjamin, and Levi. The rest of the tribes, ten in number, were in the territory of the Kingdom of Israel.

Israel was both more numerous and more prosperous than its sister kingdom, Judah. In spiritual terms, however, Judah was the stronger. The sanctity and influence of the Holy Temple inspired most of the people of Judah, most of the time, with the passionate monotheism that had been the hallmark of the Jewish people since the days of Moses. Yahweh was their God, and despite occasional aberrations when they were tempted to worship the pagan gods of their Canaanite neighbors, they believed Him to be Sovereign of the universe. The great prophets Isaiah, Amos, and Jeremiah helped fortify the monotheistic environment in the Kingdom of Judah through perpetual preaching and exhortation.

However, in the northern Kingdom of Israel—if the biblical evidence is to be taken seriously—the Israelites were very susceptible to the worship of alien gods, especially the god of their Phoenician neighbors, Baal, who was the god of the rain and of the harvest.

Ahab succeeded his father, King Omri, and shortly thereafter married Jezebel, daughter of the Phoenician King of Sidon. Jezebel, who was tyrannical and zealously devoted to Baal, proceeded to murder the prophets of Yahweh and to mandate the worship of Baal throughout the Kingdom of Israel. At this point, Elijah made his unceremonious first appearance to tell Ahab that a drought was at hand and

that "there will be no dew or rain except at my bidding."
The zealotry of Jezebel met its match in that of Elijah, who
was to say somewhat later: "I am moved by zeal for the
Lord, the God of hosts, for the Israelites have forsaken
Your covenant, torn down Your altars, and put Your
prophets to the sword. I alone am left, and they are out to
take my life."

## Elijah the Zealot

At the time, Elijah was indeed running for his life. Jezebel
had ordered his execution as a consequence of one of
the most melodramatic scenes of the Hebrew Bible, a scene
staged by Elijah in the presence of thousands of Israelites.
He had persuaded all the prophets of Baal to engage in a
contest with him alone, a contest to determine who was the
true God, Baal or Yahweh. Two altars were erected, one to
the Phoenician god and the other to the God of Israel. The
prophets of Baal slaughtered a bull and placed him on their
altar. Elijah did the same for his altar. Wood, but no fire,
was laid upon the altars. Speaking to Baal's prophets, Elijah
said:

> "You will invoke your god by name and I will invoke the
> Lord by name and let us agree the god who responds with
> fire, that one is God."

The prophets of Baal shouted themselves hoarse with the cry "O Baal answer us!" But there was no response. They hopped and danced and gashed themselves with knives in the frantic hope of evoking their god's response. Still there was none. This went on until the sun was past its zenith. Then the prophet Elijah stepped forward and said:

> "O Lord, God of Abraham, Isaac and Israel! Let it be known today that you are God in Israel and that I am your servant, and that I have done all these things at your bidding. Answer me, O Lord, answer me, that this people may know that You, O Lord, are God . . ."
>
> Then fire from the Lord descended and consumed the burnt offering, the wood, the stones, and the earth; and it licked up the water that was in the trench. When they saw this, all the people flung themselves on their faces and cried out, "The Lord alone is God: The Lord alone is God!"

At this point Elijah would have been well advised to moderate his zealotry and to rest content. Alas, he followed the climactic event with the gratuitous slaughter of all the prophets of Baal, as if in retaliation for the savagery of Jezebel. So Jezebel set out her gendarmes to slay Elijah. The prophet fled, filled with bitterness that he remained a marked man despite his monumental demonstration of the omnipotence of the God of Israel. He sought for a sign that God was still with him, and his feet carried him after a journey of forty days and forty nights to the mountain of God at Horeb. Horeb is identical with Mount Sinai, where the man called the Father of Prophets, Moses, spent forty days and nights in the epochal communion with God that brought Judaism into the world.

Elijah spent the night in a cave at Horeb waiting for a sign from God:

> And lo, the Lord passed by. There was a great and mighty wind, splitting mountains and shattering rocks by the power of the Lord; but the Lord was not in the wind. After the wind—an earthquake, but the Lord was not in the earthquake. After the earthquake—fire; but the Lord was not in the fire. And after the fire, a still small voice . . .

This magnificent passage shows that God is not about killing and mayhem and destruction. To think so is the ultimate blasphemy. God is the "still small voice," gently communicating its love and its truth to the ears that would listen.

An English poet, Thomas Campbell (1777–1854), caught the spirit of Elijah at Mount Horeb in his "Elijah's Interview":

> *On Horeb's rock the prophet stood,—*
> *The Lord before him passed;*
> *A hurricane in angry mood*
> *Swept by him strong and fast;*
> *The forest fell before its force,*
> *The rocks were shivered in its course,*
> *God was not in the blast:*

*Elijah Taken Up to Heaven in a Chariot of Fire*

'Twas but the whirlwind of his breath,
Announcing danger, wreck, and death.

It ceased. The air grew mute,—a cloud
    Came muffling up the sun;
When through the mountain, deep and loud,
An earthquake thundered on;
The frighted eagle sprang in air,
The wolf ran howling from his lair,—
    God was not in the storm;—
'Twas but the rolling of his car,—
The trampling of his steeds from far.

'Twas still again,—and Nature stood
    And calmed her ruffled frame;
When swift from heaven a fiery flood
    To earth devouring came;
Down to the depth the ocean fled,—
The sick'ning sun looked wan and dead,
    Yet God filled not the flame;—
'Twas but the terror of his eye,
That lightened through the troubled sky.

At last a voice, all still and small,
    Rose sweetly on the ear;
Yet rose so shrill and clear, that all
    In heaven and earth might hear.
It spoke of peace, it spoke of love,
It spoke as angels, speak above,
    And God himself was there!
For O, it was a Father's voice
That bade the trembling heart rejoice!

In effect, God fired Elijah at Horeb, ordering him to anoint Elisha, son of Shapat, as his successor. The Supreme Judge had here followed the precedent He set with Moses, who had to appoint Joshua as his successor because Moses had lost his temper.

## Elijah Transported

≈≈≈≈≈≈≈≈≈≈≈≈≈≈≈≈≈≈≈≈≈≈≈≈

Chapter 2 of 2 Kings begins with these words: "When the Lord was about to take Elijah up to heaven in a whirlwind . . ." It seems clear that cause and effect are subtly hinted here. The cause of Elijah's seemingly premature ascension to heaven is to be found in the tumultuous, whirlwindlike career of an extraordinary prophet who had yet to learn, however, of the still small voice. He would learn it among the angels. Jewish tradition saw to that. Indeed, he would become an angel himself, an angel whose purpose could be subsumed under the heading "Unfinished Earthly Business."

≈ ≈ ≈

# The Heavenly Elijah

~~~~~~~~~~~~~~~~~~~~~~~~~~~~~~~~~~~~~~~~~~~~~~~~~

But Elijah's ascension to heaven was not a free ride. His arrival there, according to Kabbalistic lore, was fiercely opposed by the Angel of Death with the argument that all humans were subject to his ultimate jurisdiction. God said to the Angel of Death: "Elijah is not like other men. He is even able to eliminate you should you challenge him." God then gave His consent to an Elijah–Angel of Death showdown. It would have ended with the demise of the Grim Reaper had not God held Elijah back. How well was Elijah to be taught in heaven from the first that even killing the killer himself is not the way of God. On the contrary, the role for which God had cast Elijah was to conserve, to help, and to save. "Be the guardian angel of my children forever and make yourself known as My messenger throughout the world" was God's charge to the new arrival. He was even given a new angelic name, Sandalfon, and in that capacity one of Elijah's chief duties was to design garlands for God out of the prayers offered to Him on earth.

In the literature of the Talmud, Elijah emerges as champion of underdogs and innocents, as friend of those in need, and, especially, as the guardian of good and pious folk in the face of serious dangers. He appears in an impressive variety of guises, depending on his particular mission.

～ ～ ～

THE SAGES OF the Talmud were frequent targets of Rome's punitive measures against the Jews of Eretz Israel. Frequently the goodwill of the Roman Emperor was sought through lavish gifts. One such gift, as the Talmud relates, was carried in a box by the saintly Nahum of Gamzu. On the way Nahum stopped overnight at an inn where thieves removed the valuable content of the box, replacing it with dirt. Innocently, the saintly man offered the box to the Emperor, who, upon opening it, flew into a rage and ordered Nahum's execution. Enter Elijah, in the guise of a court official. He said: "Perhaps the earth in this box is of the kind Abraham used to fight his enemies. When cast into the enemies' face it was more destructive than any other weapons." The dirt was then employed in a battle (conveniently) at hand with spectacular results. Nahum was showered with gifts and honorably sent on his way.

A Yiddish folk saying has it that "if God wills it, an ordinary broomstick will shoot bullets" (*ahz gott vil shist ah bezim*). In the setting of Nahum of Gamzu—a teacher of the great Rabbi Akiba—during which the valiant Simon Bar Cokhba was secretly organizing a Jewish rebellion against the Romans, such an Elijah miracle story fits quite well. The Jews, without conventional arms, were really no match for the Romans. The Bar Cokhba enterprise seemed foolhardy and hopeless. Rabbis like Jochanan bar Torta were outspoken in denouncing what they saw as impending suicidal catastrophe. Still, Akiba, the greatest Rabbi of the age, proclaimed Bar Cokhba the Messiah and felt their faith would overcome any shortage of armament. Alas, Bar Torta proved to be right: During the years of the Bar Cokhba Revolt (132–135 C.E.), 585,000 Jews were slaughtered by the Romans, according to the historian Dio Cassius. And Elijah did not appear.

Elijah and Rabbi Akiba had had an encounter during the Rabbi's early years of physical hardships. Akiba, so the story goes, had once been an untutored shepherd working for the immensely wealthy Kalba Savua. The rich man's daughter, Rachel, fell in love with Akiba and married him over her father's objections. She was immediately disowned and, consequently, led a life of extreme privation with her husband. Akiba felt deeply for her, understanding the sacrifices she'd made to be with him. During nights of biting cold, they had nothing more than straw on a dirt floor for bedding. On one such night Akiba's heart was heavy with sorrow, when suddenly Elijah appeared at the entrance to their shabby hut in the guise of a tattered beggar. He spoke in tearful supplication: "O good people, I beg you for a small bundle of straw. My wife has just given birth and I need straw to make a bed for her and the child." Upon hearing so sad a story, Rachel and Akiba put their own woes into a more positive perspective. It goes without saying that the poor man got his straw. But what he gave the donors was so much more than he received.

# God's Helping Hand

~~~~~~~~~~~~~~~~~~~~~~~~~~~~~~~~~~~~~~~~

Elijah, the prophet-angel, is often seen as giving of himself in total unselfishness. There is the tale of the poor man with a large family who, having reached the limit of his afflictions, cried out to God for mercy and compassion, else death would be preferable. Suddenly Elijah appeared, saying: "Sell me as a slave and provide for your family with the proceeds." The poor man had to be persuaded to do so. He sold Elijah to a prince for a princely sum. The prince had plans to build a palace. His newly acquired slave volunteered that he was an expert architect. The prince promised Elijah that if he would complete the structure within six months he would have his freedom. That night Elijah offered a prayer to God and, as dawn broke, the palace stood complete in regal splendor. The prince was overjoyed, but when he looked for the "architect"-slave in order to reward him properly, he was nowhere to be found. The prince then realized that, however briefly, he had had an angel in his service.

A poetic version of this legend composed by Rabbi Jesse ben Mordecai has become part of the liturgy of the Havdalah service, which comes at the end of the Sabbath. Interestingly, that service is dominated by the presence of Elijah. After the blessing marking the beginning of the workaday week is recited over the wine and the Havdalah candle, a hymn is sung. The refrain is:

*Elijah the Prophet*
*Elijah the Tishbite*
*Elijah the Gileadite—*
*Very soon in our own day*
*He will be coming our way*
*In company with Messiah*
*Descendant of David.*

## Redressing Injustice

~~~~~~~~~~~~~~~~~~~~~~~~~~~~~~~~~~~

The outcry of human suffering had always reached Elijah during his career as a mortal. To redress injustice was a consuming passion for the man from Gilead. Naboth the Jezrealite owned a vineyard that adjoined the palace of King Ahab and Ahab offered to buy at a very good price. Naboth refused, saying: "The Lord forbid that I should give up to you what I have inherited from my fathers!" Ahab was dejected by the unexpected stand of Naboth to the point of losing his appetite and taking to his bed. Learning of the Naboth business from her husband, Jezebel had trumped-up charges of treason leveled against Naboth by two venal scoundrels. Equally corrupt judges then sentenced Naboth to death by stoning. Jezebel then advised her husband to take possession of Naboth's vineyard, which the King promptly did.

> Then the word of the Lord came to Elijah the Tishbite: "Go down and confront King Ahab of Israel . . . Say to him: 'Thus said the Lord: Would you murder and take possession? Thus said the Lord: In the very place where the dogs lapped up Naboth's blood, the dogs will lap up your blood too.' " . . .
>
> And the Lord has also spoken concerning Jezebel: "The dogs shall devour Jezebel in the field of Jezreel."
>
> (1 KINGS 21:23)

To confront power without regard for the consequences—to restore justice—was the hallmark of the prophets of Israel—and the essence of Elijah's persona, both as human and as angel. The worst of sins, as he perceived it, was closing our eyes to misery. According to the Talmud (Baba Batra 76), he broke off his relationship with a friend who had built a wall around his capacious home to block out the sounds of pleading by itinerant beggars.

"A man's a man for a' that" was a tenet Elijah held dear. Considerations of class, background, or appearance played no role whatever in his ethical scheme. He taught an unforgettable lesson to the learned teacher Eliezer, son of the great Simon bar Yohai. Rabbi Eliezer was rather haughty and condescending toward people who did not meet his standards of scholarship or aesthetics.

> Once, on returning from the academy, he walked along the sea-beach very pleased with himself because of his profound Torah-learning. He met a very homely man who

greeted him with the words: "Peace be with you, Rabbi."
Eliezer curtly responded: "How homely you are. Are all the
people of your town as homely as you are?" "I do not
know" was the reply, "but your complaint should be addressed to my Creator."

(BABYLONIAN TALMUD, author's translation)

The homely man proved to be Elijah in one of his multi-
faceted guises. It took genuine regret and urgent pleading
by Rabbi Eliezer to secure the forgiveness of the man he
had humiliated. To Elijah, every human, since he was created in God's image, was a king—unless, of course, like
Ahab and Jezebel, the godly image was self-effaced.

## Elijah and the Messiah

The Elijah concept of humility embraced his own understanding of the Messiah's whereabouts. Rabbi Joshua
ben Levi, whom we have already met, was a favorite of
Elijah, and they often visited with each other. At one time
Rabbi Joshua begged Elijah to secure him an interview
with the Messiah. Elijah brought him to the outskirts of
Rome, where Joshua found the Messiah among bedraggled
paupers. The Rabbi greeted the Messiah with the words
"Peace be with you, my teacher and guide!" The Messiah
returned the greeting. The Rabbi then asked him when he
would finally appear to do his work of redemption. The

Messiah answered: "Today." Later Elijah explained to Rabbi Joshua that the Messiah is ready to arrive any day, provided that the people of Israel proved themselves worthy by doing the work they were commissioned to do by God. Clearly, in the context of Messiah among bedraggled paupers, the lesson was that before he could arrive, the victims of human neglect and callousness must be released from their straits.

ELIJAH THE PROPHET-ANGEL looms largest in the lore of the Jewish people as the forerunner of the Messiah. He is to prepare the way for the Messiah's arrival by inducing Israel to repent and by laying the foundations for peace and justice that are the preconditions of salvation. Three ringing proclamations will be uttered by Elijah in Israel on the three days immediately preceding the advent of the Messiah. On the first day the words will be: "Now peace will come upon earth!" On the second: "Good will come upon earth!" Finally, on the third day: "Salvation will come upon earth!" Then the Archangel Michael will blow the trumpet and Elijah will again appear, this time to introduce the Messiah in the flesh.

The Messiah will have Elijah blow the trumpet, and, at the first sound, the primal light, which shone before the week of the Creation, will reappear; at the second sound the dead will arise, and with the swiftness of wind assemble around the Messiah from all corners of the earth; at the third sound, the Shekhinah will become visible to all; the mountains will be razed at the fourth sound, and the Temple will stand in complete perfection as (the Prophet) Ezekiel described it.

During the reign of peace, Elijah will be one of the eight princes forming the cabinet of the Messiah. Even the coming of the great judgment day will not end his activity. On that day the children of the wicked who had to die in infancy on account of the sins of their fathers will be found among the just, while their fathers will be ranged on the other side. The babes will implore their fathers to come to them, but God will not permit it. Then Elijah will go to the little ones, and teach them how to plead in behalf of their fathers. They will stand before God and say: "Is not the measure of good, the mercy of God, larger than the measure of chastisements?; If, then, we died for the sins of our fathers, should they not now for our sakes be granted the good, and be permitted to join us in Paradise?" God will give assent to their pleadings, and Elijah will have fulfilled the word of the Prophet Malachi; he will have brought back the fathers to the children.[1]

Reconciliation, restitution, rejuvenation, restoration, revelation, and, ultimately, redemption are the six *R*'s of Elijah's pedagogy. The most daunting of all educational challenges was placed upon the shoulders of the Tishbite, who continued his superhuman work as an angel.

Elijah is the supreme example in Jewish lore of the ideal

relationship between the earthly and the heavenly, between the human and the angelic. In the Jewish faith the two spheres are interlaced. Heavenly activity must alleviate earthly suffering. For a human to engage in this work, he must arm himself with angelic qualities.

Elijah, the prophet-angel, shows the way.

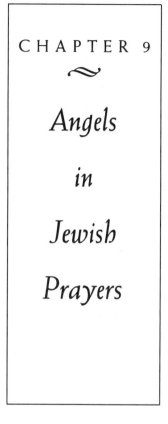

CHAPTER 9

~

*Angels*

*in*

*Jewish*

*Prayers*

## Evolution of the Jewish Liturgy

~ ~ ~ ~ ~ ~ ~ ~ ~ ~ ~ ~ ~ ~ ~ ~ ~ ~ ~ ~ ~

The Jewish prayer books—the *Siddur* and the *Machzor* —are made up largely of prayers composed during the Talmudic era (the first five centuries C.E.). The Rabbis of the Talmud provided for both the organization and the content of the standard daily and holiday liturgies. The very first tractate of the Talmud—*Berakhot*, or "Blessings"—contains the basic ingredients that comprise traditional Jewish liturgy to this very day.

Following the Talmudic era—from the sixth through the twelfth centuries C.E.—a good deal of religious poetry was produced by some very gifted souls. In Palestine there were people like Yosei ben Yosei, Yannai, and Elazar Kalir, who devoted their lifetimes to composing religious poetry around the structure of the liturgy in the Talmud. They made liberal use of angels in their work, often by way of commenting on the sorry plight of the Children of Israel under the dominion of cruel nations, a plight of which God in heaven was aware and would in due course send His angels to rectify.

With the efflorescence of Jewish mysticism during the twelfth and thirteenth centuries in Spain and in southern France, Kabbalistic prayers made their way into the liturgy, encapsulating much of the Kabbalah's esoteric lore and incurring the condemnation of many rabbis and other religionists who saw in them heretical ideas, especially in the tendency to personify angels. With the charismatic teaching of Rabbi Isaac Luria in sixteenth-century Palestine, Sabbath hymns that were saturated with angels and other mysteries of the Kabbalah were incorporated into the liturgy.

# The Role of Angels in Jewish Prayer

~ ~ ~ ~ ~ ~ ~ ~ ~ ~ ~ ~ ~ ~ ~ ~ ~ ~ ~ ~

Even with the proliferation of angels in the liturgy, prayers were never addressed to angels. On some occasions angels were asked to bring prayers to the Throne of God. Traces of Kabbalistic ideas are found in medieval poems that speak of angels as "deliverers of prayers for God's compassion" (*makhnisei rahamim*), some of which were incorporated into the Jewish prayer book. In the early stages of medieval Jewish mysticism the figure of the angel Sandalfon—a fiery angel in the "seventh heaven" who was always close to God's Throne and who brought the prayers of humans before Him—emerged. In this capacity, Sandalfon is celebrated in the medieval religious poetry known as *piyyut*. Solomon ibn Gabirol, one of Spanish Jewry's greatest poets (eleventh century), portrayed Sandalfon as the angel who bears the prayers of Israel to its God.

The Jewish prayer book—the *Siddur*—makes it absolutely clear that the angels themselves as creatures of God offer their homage to Him in hymns of praise that they constantly sing. The daily morning service includes the prayer from Nehemiah 6:

> You are the Lord, you alone. You created the heavens and
> the heaven of heavens with all their host, the earth and all
> the things upon it, the seas and all that is in them; and you

preserve them all. The host of the heavens (the angelic beings) worships you.

The central prayer, the *Sh'ma*, which affirms the unity of God in the Deuteronomic words "Hear, O Israel, the Lord our God is One," is preceded by a passage placing angels in a perspective that nullifies any possible notion that they might be independent celestial forces:

> We bless you, our Stronghold, our King and Redeemer, Creator of holy beings. May your name forever be praised, our King, Creator of ministering angels, all of whom stand at the heights of the universe and reverently declaim, together and with one voice the words of the living God, the everlasting King. All of them are beloved, all of them are pure, all of them are strong; they all perform with awe and reverence the will of their Creator; they all open their mouth with holiness and purity, with song and melody, while they bless and praise, glorify and revere, sanctify and acclaim the name of the great, mighty and awesome God and King . . .

Even the heavily laden angelology of the *Zohar*, linchpin of the Kabbalah, stresses the exclusivity of God as destination of all faith and prayer. A beautiful prayer from the *Zohar* has been incorporated into almost all editions of the *Siddur*. It reads in part:

I am the servant of the Holy One, blessed be He, before whom and before whose glorious Torah I bow at all times. Not in man do I put my trust, nor do I rely on any angel, but only in the God of Heaven who is the God of truth, whose Torah is truth and whose Prophets are truth, and who performs multifarious deeds of goodness and truth.

In many prayer books, the greeting to the Angels of Peace preceding the Sabbath eve meal is followed by a deeply moving invocation to the "Master of all Worlds," which refers to the blessed angels who do the will of God. The prayer pleads:

I beg you, O King, who is the King of Kings, bid your angels, the angels who minister to you, to consider me with compassion and to bless me as they enter my home on our holy day.

The fiery angels of the vision of Isaiah—the Seraphim—surround the Throne of God, calling to each other:

"Holy, holy, holy, the Lord of Hosts!
His presence fills all the earth!"
(ISAIAH 6:3)

This has become the heart of the prayer of sanctification (the *Kedushah*), which is a vital part of every Jewish prayer service. There are several versions of this prayer, depending upon the time of day it is recited or whether it is a weekday or the Sabbath or a festival day. In its latter form it reads:

*Angels in Jewish Prayers* ∼ 225

We revere and sanctify You in the words of the assembly of holy seraphim who hallow your name in the sanctuary, as it is written by your prophet:

*"And one calls to the other,*
   *'Holy, holy, holy!*
    *The Lord of Hosts!*
*His presence fills all the earth.' "*
   His presence fills the universe; His ministering angels ask one another: "Where is His glorious presence?" They respond to each other: "Blessed is the Presence of the Lord, in his place" [which is, as said just above, the whole of the universe].

AN INSIGHT INTO the Jewish conception of prayer and the involvement of angels in it is afforded by the same chapter of Isaiah. Following the "Holy, Holy, Holy" of the Seraphim in Isaiah's theophany, the prophet is seized with trembling. He cries out:

   "Woe is me; I am lost!
   For I am a man of unclean lips
   And I live among a people
   Of unclean lips,
   Yet my own eyes have beheld
   the King Lord of Hosts."

   Then one of the seraphs flew over to me with a
   live coal, which he had taken from the altar

with a pair of tongs. He touched it to my
lips and declared,

"Now that this has touched your lips
Your guilt shall depart
And your sin be purged away."

(ISAIAH 6)

To the truly God-fearing person, the thought of approaching the Almighty Himself is daunting. Job's friend Bildad the Shuhite asked rhetorically:

"How can man be in the right before God?
How can one born of woman be cleared of guilt?
Even the moon is not bright
And the stars are not pure in His sight.
How much less man, a worm,
The son-of-man, a maggot."

Bildad's friend Eliphaz the Temanite heard a voice saying:

"Can mortals be acquitted by God?
Can man be cleared by his Maker?
If He cannot trust his own servants,
And casts reproach on His angels,
How much less those who dwell in houses of clay,
Whose origin is dust?"

We can understand how Isaiah's sense of overwhelming awe in the presence of God renders him virtually speechless. For a prophet, that would be a serious shortcoming indeed. So the Seraph, the fiery angel, becomes his interlocutor, and, to begin with, he purges Isaiah of his feelings of inadequacy. The rest of the prophet's vision finds him in direct dialogue with God. The angels in the Jewish prayer book would seem to serve a similar purpose: The example of their ongoing praise for the Lord encourages mortals to approach their Maker with their own prayers of praise or thanks or expostulation.

In Kabbalistic teaching, as we have already noted, angels are created by the deeds of man in accordance with the nature of the deed. On one of the holiest days of the Jewish calendar year—Rosh Hashanah, the beginning of the year —the mitzvah of sounding the Shofar, or the ram's horn, is ordained in the Torah. Though there are a number of explanations for this, the clearest of them is that the Shofar's sounds are wake-up calls reminding the Jew that Rosh Hashanah is the day of judgment and that he must therefore search his soul for the purpose of its purification so that he might be inscribed for the coming year in God's book of life. One of the powerful prayers of the day, the *Untaneh Tokef*, includes the following description of the "day of awe and dread":

> A great shofar is sounded. A still small voice is heard. The angels hurry to and fro. Fear and trembling seize them, and they cry out: Lo, the day of Judgment! to arraign the heavenly host in judgment, for in Your sight not even they are

pure. All mortals, too, are caused by You to pass before you as a flock of sheep. As a shepherd counts his herd and makes each sheep pass beneath his staff, so do You record and number and take account of every living soul, setting a limit to every creature's life and passing sentence upon all of them.

The idea that even angels must pass divine muster makes it easier for mere mortals to be hopeful. After all, not even angels are without fault. Let humans then confess their faults on this day of judgment: It will do their souls good, and it will please the Supreme Judge.

In keeping with Kabbalistic thought, the very sounds of the Shofar, if produced with the proper intent and in pious concentration, send angels upward to the Throne of God. They then serve as advocates on behalf of the congregation in which the Shofar is sounded. The Kabbalists introduced prayers to that effect following every series of the various Shofar sounds, such as:

> May it be your will, O Lord our God and God of our fathers, that the angels emerging from the sounds of the shofar will ascend to your Throne of Glory and will speak kindly in our behalf to help in the atonement of all our sins.

Because the Jewish mystics were ever conscious of the presence of Satan, the adversary, even in the midst of their prayers and especially on the day of judgment, Rosh Hashanah—it was his assignment to be their prosecutor—

they added an important reason for the sounding of the Shofar, namely, to confound and confuse Satan so that he would fail in his adversarial mission. They also appended as a prefatory prayer to sounding the Shofar six verses from different sections of the Book of Psalms, the first letters of which spell out (in Hebrew) the acrostic *KRA SATAN*, whose meaning is "rend Satan asunder."

The conflict between the Angels of Mercy—Sandalfon's army—and Satan's host on Rosh Hashanah and Yom Kippur, the days of awe and judgment, is dramatically expressed in the *Hineni*, a prayer in which the Cantor, leading the congregation, pleads with God that He "rebuke Satan and keep him from blocking the ascent of my prayers," and, on the other hand:

> May it be your will, God of Abraham, God of Isaac and God of Jacob, the great, mighty and revered, the God supreme over all . . . that all the angels who are assigned to prayers convey my prayer before the throne of your glory and spread it before you. (I ask this) for the sake of all the righteous, the pure and the upright and for the sake of the glory of your name which is mighty and awesome. For you heed the prayer of your people Israel with compassion.

~ ~ ~

# Prayers as Angels

~ ~ ~ ~ ~ ~ ~ ~ ~ ~ ~ ~ ~ ~ ~ ~ ~ ~ ~ ~ ~

In a deeper sense, prayers are angels and Sandalfon is a metaphor for them, no more. A prayer uttered to God from the *heart* of the petitioner will sprout wings and fly heavenward. There are many stories about the prayers of truly pious people: Some Hasidic masters supposedly generated visible flames around their bodies as they prayed, while others caused such a commotion in the heavens with their prayers that the angelic hosts were forced to stop whatever they were doing and listen. The mystic figure of Honi the Circle Maker, a legendary personage of the first century, is described as drawing a ring about himself in a year of severe drought and, waving his finger heavenward, praying: "Dear Lord, let it be known that I will not leave this ring until You put an end to the drought that is killing Your people!" And the rains came.

IN THE SUMMER of 1952, peace talks between the Americans and the North Koreans were in progress at Panmunjom. I was stationed near Taegu, not too far away, as a chaplain for the Tenth Army Corps. From my headquarters I set forth every morning in a jeep on the way to units miles distant, where I led Jewish soldiers in prayer. Because I covered about three hundred miles every week along bumpy and narrow mountain roads, someone painted the legend

"Rough-Ridin' Rabbi" on the back of the jeep. Above the words was a rough sketch of a Jew wearing a prayer shawl with his hands outstretched.

The week before I was to return to the States, I held my last service for the smallest of the congregations—four men and one woman (an army nurse), who also were the farthest to reach. For months our attendance had been 100 percent. At the last service, one of the men was missing—as I soon learned, permanently so. He had been killed by a land mine three days earlier, and his body was already aboard a transport plane on the way home.

We could not get into a prayer mode in any routine fashion. The prayer book somehow failed to say what was in our hearts. The nurse, a lieutenant named Sarah, spoke: "Does God really listen to prayer, Rabbi?" And she wept. Almost immediately the rest of us broke into tears. The tears flowed freely, punctuated only by sobs that still ring in my ears. When all was quiet, I said, "Sarah, I think you have the answer to your question." I asked them to join me in the traditional memorial prayer, the *Kaddish*. Our service ended. I remained in the tent for about an hour talking to the men. Sarah had had to leave.

I came back to get into my jeep. I stopped short. The outstretched hands of the Jew in the prayer shawl had been replaced by wings. Sarah was a few feet away. "Drive back carefully, Rabbi," she said. And she waved farewell.

CHAPTER 10

*Angels*

*in*

*Modern*

*Dress*

## Angels Today?

Now, we look at angels and devils not in the way we think about Santa Claus or ghosts, but as symbols that help to define the human experience. Such terms as *id* and *ego* in psychology, for example, or such names as Clio and Erato in literature, may not represent concrete, palpable beings, but they do convey important aspects of our being.

So is it with angels and devils in the Jewish tradition. The angelic and the diabolic phenomena within ourselves are still very much a part of human nature. We remain in the company of our angels.

Several modern Jewish writers bring the role of angels into the twentieth century.

## Steinsaltz's Angels

≈≈≈≈≈≈≈≈≈≈≈≈≈≈≈≈≈≈≈≈≈≈≈≈

Some twelve years ago, Adin Steinsaltz wrote *The Thirteen Petalled Rose*,[1] a popular exposition of the Kabbalah in which he summarizes the four worlds comprising the Kabbalistic system. The topmost and most spiritual is the world of Emanation. Beneath it is the world of Creation. Below that are the worlds of Formation and Action or Doing—the universe we inhabit.

Within these worlds, there are two kinds of angels: those who were created by God at the very beginning and who in turn became part of the process of the Creation, and those who are constantly created out of man's thoughts, deeds, and actions.

Every *mitzvah* (religious act) that a man does is not only an act of transformation in the material world; it is also a spiritual act, sacred in itself. And this aspect of concentrated spirituality and holiness in the *mitzvah* is the chief component of that which becomes an angel.

But human actions could work the other way as well:

. . . just as there are holy angels . . . there are also destructive angels, called "devils" or "demons" who are the emanations of the connection of man with those aspects of reality which are the opposite of holiness. Here, too, the actions of man . . . created angels, but angels of another sort . . . These are hostile angels that may be part of a lower world or even of a higher, more spiritual world—this last because even though they do not belong to the realm of holiness . . . there is a mutual interpenetration and influence between the holy and the not-holy.

In a very apt phrase, Steinsaltz describes the subversive, destructive angels created by human evildoing as "the objectification of malevolence." Angels of both kinds, good and evil, accompany man throughout his life. After all, they are his handiwork. Angels and devils are real enough to Steinsaltz, but only in the metaphorical sense.

Steinsaltz offers his own definition:

Angels are beings in the world that is the domain of emotion and feeling; and since this is the case, the substantial quality of an angel may be an impulse or a drive—say, an inclination in the direction of love or a seizure of fear, or pity or the like.

Steinsaltz sees "working" angels as manifestations of aspects of the human personality and reflections of human behavior. The angel is the messenger of God, to be sure. The Hebrew word for angel, *Malakh*, does mean "messenger." But the message is one of our own making.

## The Elusive Angel

~ ~ ~ ~ ~ ~ ~ ~ ~ ~ ~ ~ ~ ~ ~ ~ ~ ~ ~ ~ ~ ~ ~

The other thinkers we shall now briefly consider are Franz Kafka, Walter Benjamin, and Gershom Scholem. Robert Alter's illuminating book, *Necessary Angels*,[2] published in 1991, raises the question of some modern perspectives on the matter of angels.

In 1921, Benjamin acquired a Paul Klee painting, *Angelus Novus*, that, according to his good friend Scholem, he kept for the rest of his life as "a kind of spiritual talisman and focus for meditation." Benjamin bequeathed the painting to Scholem, and it hung in the living room of the Scholem home until 1989, when Scholem's widow placed it in the Israel Museum. Here, Benjamin describes the work:

A Klee painting named "Angelus Novus" shows an angel looking as though he is about to move away from something he is fixedly contemplating. His eyes are staring, his mouth is open, his wings are spread; this is how one pictures the angel of history. His face is turned toward the past. Where we perceive a chain of events he sees one single catastrophe which keeps piling wreckage upon wreckage and hurls it in front of his feet. The angel would like to stay, awaken the dead, and make whole what has been smashed. But a storm is blowing from Paradise, it has got caught in his wings with such violence that the angel can no longer close them. The storm irresistibly propels him into the future to which his back is turned, while the pile of debris before him grows skyward. This storm is what we call progress.

Benjamin's angel is the allegorical representation of a humanity that continues to be blown farther and farther away from the Garden of Eden by the relentless storm of corruption and violence created by humankind. *Angelus Novus* is not new at all. It is the symbol of the continuation of man's self-inflicted expulsion from paradise and of his irremediable retreat into the netherparts of *Gehenna*.

Benjamin lived long enough to witness the beginning of the mass murders by the SS and the *Einsatzgruppen*. How can one talk of progress when the end result of theology, science, and the Age of Enlightenment was the advent of Hitler, Eichmann, and Mengele? "This storm is what we call progress," he writes, in utter disenchantment and despair.

Scholem's reactions to the *Angelus Novus* were expressed in a poem he included in a letter he sent to Benjamin. In the poem the angel himself speaks. He is, he says, *ein Engelsmann* ("an angelman"). He has been sent on a mission of revelation to humanity but longs to return to his celestial dwelling. The nature of the revelation is not made clear, even what he is supposed to represent is obscure:

> "I am an unsymbolic thing,
> Meaning what I am,
> You turn in vain the magic ring,
> I don't have any sense."

Through the angel, God is speaking to humankind. But what the angel is saying is not clear. We are left with the question: Is the angel unclear because ultimately God surpasses human understanding or is he unclear because humanity turns a deaf ear to his message? Like Scholem's lifelong study of the Kabbalah and Jewish mysticism, the *Angelus Novus* is steeped in a mystery.

FRANZ KAFKA'S DIARY ENTRY for June 25, 1914, contains what may have been an outline for a story he never published. In his room the author perceives a tremor in the ceiling as if something is trying to break through. An arm holding a silver sword thrusts out from above and the narrator recognizes it as "a vision intended for my liberation." In a spasm of temperament, the narrator jumps on the table and pulls the electric fixture from the ceiling, which immediately breaks open:

> In the dim light, still at great height, I had judged it badly, an angel in bluish-violet robes girt with gold chords sank slowly down on great white silken-shining wings, the sword in its raised arm thrust out horizontally. "An angel, then," I thought, "it has been flying towards me all the day and in my disbelief I did not know it. Now it will speak to me." I lowered my eyes. When I raised them again the angel was still there, it is true, hanging rather far under the ceiling (which had closed again), but it was no living angel, only a painted wooden figurehead off the prow of some ship, one of the kind that hangs from the ceiling in sailors' taverns, nothing more.
>
> The hilt of the sword was made in such a way as to hold candles and catch the dripping tallow. I had pulled the electric light down. I didn't want to remain in the dark. There was still one candle left, so I got up on a chair, stuck the candle into the hilt of the sword, lit it, and then sat late into the night under the angel's faint flame.

Kafka's hallucinatory experience is a brilliant depiction of the sublime and the ridiculous in the worlds of aspiration and reality that the poetic soul inhabits simultaneously. The poet aspires to an angelic epiphany, to a terrestrial world suffused with heavenly light. But the reality is that the angelic dispenser of light turns out to be a cheap figurehead from the prow of a ship that no longer sails the open seas. Even worse, the angel bears a sword in his hand. Is he the cherub guarding paradise against Adam and Eve's reentry, or is he, in fact, the Angel of Death? The image of the whole is certainly Kafkaesque. Whatever the case, the narrator refuses to despair. In Robert Alter's words: "If the angel exposed as a lifeless thing, cannot actively provide spiritual illumination, it can be made an implement for shedding light." Even more than that, I think, is inherent in Kafka's account. By lighting a candle within the very hilt of the angel's sword, the narrator is in a way expressing Isaiah's vision of the breaking of swords into plowshares; that is, substituting that which brings forth life for the deadly sword of the Grim Reaper. "Kafka's silent angel," writes Alter, ". . . is made, through a willed act of human intervention, to hold a candle for the man to whom it has appeared."

## Angel of Light

~ ~ ~ ~ ~ ~ ~ ~ ~ ~ ~ ~ ~ ~ ~ ~ ~ ~ ~ ~ ~ ~ ~

The angel as light giver has survived in the modern literature of the Jews despite the near-extinction of light experienced by the Jewish people during what Lucy Dawidowicz has titled "The War Against the Jews," the era of unprecedented evil that dominated the twelve years of Satan, 1933 to 1945. The thought of angels during this period is evocative of the Psalmodic passage "Yea, though I walk through the valley of the shadow of death I will fear no evil for Thou are with me . . . Surely goodness and mercy will follow me all the days of my life." Surely it is remarkable to think of goodness and mercy in the valley of the shadow of death.

The first three stories are from Schwartz's *Gates to the New City*. The fourth—by the great Yiddish master, Isaac Leib Peretz—is from a translation of his stories by Maurice Samuel in his book *Prince of the Ghetto*.

In his story "The Eden Angel,"[3] Nachmann Rapp captures a vision of Adam and Eve both before and after they eat the Forbidden Fruit. In their state of innocence they wandered about the Garden of Eden neither happy nor sad.

> Days and weeks passed by, and they led their peaceful lives, their inane lives. The angel appointed over the Garden of Eden did not distinguish them from the other creatures of Eden, from those who walked on four roaring a hollow roar, or from those who crawled the dust in constant silence. And the miracle of man's creation which had roused the angels' wonder slowly receded and faded away.

But with their eating of the fruit, turmoil, anxiety, and fear entered the lives of Adam and Eve. Their plight drew them together and true love was born between them as they were comforted by each other's presence. They experienced the full gamut of human emotions. In truth, in the eyes of the Eden angel, they had eaten of the Tree of *Life*. Upon their expulsion from Eden the angel missed them so much he thought his heart would break. In the end, he sacrificed his own immortality in order to join the company of Adam and Eve outside of Eden, beyond the fiery sword of the cherubim who had been appointed to guard it from human reentry.

In this version of the story, Adam and Eve were humanized by their ordeal, and the Eden angel became a part of them.

Suffering and consternation as essentials of the divine plan is the theme of Martin Buber's short tale "The Angel and the World's Dominion."[4] In the story, one angel is so moved by the suffering he sees below, he begs God to entrust the administration of earth to him for one year so that he can lay the foundations for the endless well-being of all God's creatures. The Creator grants the angel's wish:

> And so a year of joy and sweetness visited the Earth. The shining angel poured the great profusion of his merciful heart over the most anguished of her children, on those who were benumbed and terrified by want. The groans of the sick and dying no longer disturbed the world's deep, surging harmony . . . The earth floated through a fecund sky that left her with the burden of new vegetation. When summer was at its height, people moved singing through the full, yellow fields; never had such abundance existed in the memory of living man.

But one cold day, late in the year, a crescendo of human anguish rose to the heavens. The angel hastened back to earth and found that the bread baked from the ample grain stored earlier in the year was unpalatable and nauseating. It tasted like clay and could not be eaten. People began to starve to death.

The angel flew back to his Maker for an explanation. God said to him:

> "Behold a truth which is known to me, and only to me from the beginning of time . . . The earth must be nourished with putrefaction and covered with shadows that its seeds may bring forth . . . Souls must be made fertile with flood and sorrow, that through them, the Great Work may be born."

## The Thirty-six Righteous

~ ~ ~ ~ ~ ~ ~ ~ ~ ~ ~ ~ ~ ~ ~ ~ ~ ~ ~ ~

The Hebrew Bible speaks of man's soul as God's candle. But not all souls are created equal. Some are irradiated with divine illumination, while the inherent light of other souls is dimmed by the behavior of the bodies they inhabit. Then there are the souls of the *Lamed-vov*, the thirty-six just people who, unheralded, unknown, and unobserved, preserve the earth from destruction through their unswerving, unfailing, unselfish deeds of love, kindness, and piety.

No soul can function without a body to call its home. In his tale "The Three Souls of Reb Aharon,"[5] Howard Schwartz tells of the housing shortages for souls that were caused by the catastrophes of the Jewish people throughout their history. A soul that remains apart from a human being is a captive soul. Jewish disasters created so many of them that the angel Raziel presented the problem to God, who decided then that certain spiritually gifted human beings would be invested with two or even three souls at one time. All who were given as many as three souls were members of the *Lamed-vov*. Reb Aharon was one of them. Shortly before his death, he had written a letter to one of his disciples that, by some accident, only reached its address nine months after Reb Aharon's death. How parlous is the lot of a bearer of three souls we learn from part of the letter's contents:

> For the souls of the Lamed-vov must contend to keep the world in existence. For if pure peace should settle in the heart of even one of the Lamed-vov, the world would sink beneath the weight of darkness. So it is that the heart of every one of the Lamed-vov holds back the waters of the Abyss. And sometimes, when the pressure of the waters grows too great to bear, the heart of a Lamed-vov breaks.

A necessary condition for a member of the *Lamed-vov* is to be utterly unaware of his own moral merit. Certainly this was true of silent Bontche, the unwitting hero of one of the best-known stories by the masterful Yiddish writer Isaac Leib Peretz.[6]

Bontche was a porter whose life was spent beneath the heavy loads he carried on his back and beneath a perpetual cloud of misfortune. Nobody ever took note of him:

> Were there less of a human hullabaloo, someone, somewhere might have heard Bontche's backbone cracking under the loads he carried; were the world in less of a hurry, someone, somewhere, might have had the time to notice that in Bontche's sunken cheeks two eyes still glimmered; and that even when he carried no pack he walked with his head bent earthward, as though already looking for his grave.

Bontche never complained, even when injustice seized him by the throat. Unlike Job, Bontche never raised his voice in protest against heaven. His own life was filled with acts of unrequited kindness, and although he was a target for the viciousness of others, the thought of retaliation never entered his mind. He was a saint but he never knew it. "He was born quietly and lived quietly, he died quietly and they buried him quietly."

But Bontche's death produced a sensation in heaven:

> The great trumpet of the Messiah pealed through the seven heavens: "Bontche is dead!" Wide-winged angels swept through space carrying the news: "Bontche has been called to the hosts of the blessed." A tumultuous joy ran through

the bowers of Eden: "Bontche is coming! Bontche! Bontche himself!" Young angels with dazzling eyes and golden wings, with silver slippers on their feet, went out to greet him . . . God Himself knew that Bontche was coming.

Bontche was terrified at what was happening around him. Surely, he thought to himself, this must be a case of mistaken identity. He feared that when he was found out he would be unceremoniously cast out from heaven. He trembled as his formal hearing began before the celestial tribunal. But as the angelic defense attorney recounted details of Bontche's career on earth, he was reassured. It is me they are talking about, after all, he thought. He heard the angel say:

> "Drenched in cold perspiration, bent double under heavy packs, suffering the cramps of hunger, he was silent. The feet of others bespattered him with mud, their spit stained him; carrying his load, he was pushed off the sidewalk among the carriages and horse-cars; death stared him in the face at every moment. He was silent . . . He was silent when his wife ran away from him and left him with a suckling infant. He was silent fifteen years later when the child had grown big enough to throw him out of the house . . . He was silent in his last agony, and silent in the moment of death. No word against God or man."

When it was the turn of the angelic prosecuting attorney to speak, he said: "He was silent. I will be silent too."
The Supreme Judge then spoke:

"Down there your silence received no reward, for that is the world of falseness and illusion. Here, in the true world, you will receive your reward . . . Take what you wish; all is yours."

"Really," Bontche asks.

"Really, really, really," they answered him.

"Well, if it's really so," answered Bontche with a smile, "then I want, every morning, a hot roll with fresh butter."

This, of course, was not what the Heavenly Court expected to hear. But then again Bontche had been in life a man with no great expectations for himself. He had lived his life as a *Lamed-vov*, one of the thirty-six saints who carry the world on their shoulders.

In Eden he's perfectly satisfied with the indulgence of a hot buttered roll for breakfast.

THE AURA OF BONTCHE the Silent has long since been dissipated by the prodigious barbarism of the last one hundred years. It is not that the angelic aspect of the human animal has been exorcised. There have lived, after all, people like Albert Schweitzer and Mother Teresa and Florence Nightingale in our midst. But the angelic has been overwhelmed by the satanic. It has seen the killing of over one hundred million people in two World Wars. It has witnessed utterly brutal and futile carnage in Korea and Vietnam. It has been through the savagery of Hiroshima and Nagasaki. It has encompassed devastation by both domestic governments and the United States to the lives of millions of people in Latin America. It has looked on as the inhumanity of apartheid accelerated. It has seen fratricidal war in Yugoslavia. It has perceived the Angel of Death in the eyes of the skeletal babies of Somalia.

And it has been the century of Auschwitz. Auschwitz was the expulsion of the angels from the garden of Adam and Eve and their replacement by Satan and Company, an establishment whose membership was open only to devils and demons. It even featured a nominally human being—a physician by profession—who came to be called "The Angel of Death."

On May 24 (1942) a new SS doctor reached Auschwitz. His name was Josef Mengele, and he had just celebrated his thirty-second birthday. His SS rank was that of Captain. Driven by the desire to advance his medical career by scientific publications, Dr. Mengele began to conduct medical experiments on living Jews whom he took from the barracks and brought to his hospital block. In many instances, amounting over a year and a half to several thousand, Mengele used the pretext of medical treatment to kill prisoners, personally injecting them with phenol, petrol, chloroform or air, or by ordering medical orderlies to do so.

From the moment of his arrival at Auschwitz, Mengele joined the other SS officers and SS doctors . . . in the "selection" of Jews reaching the railway junction from all over Europe, with a movement of the hand or a wave of the stick indicating as "unfit for work" and thus destined for immediate death in the gas-chambers all children, old people, sick, crippled and weak Jews and all pregnant women.[7]

One young man was spared from the ovens of satanism by his emigration from Poland before the start of World War II. He was a writer of prodigious talent who was destined to receive the Nobel Prize for Literature. He had met very few "angels" in his native country, a land notorious for its anti-Semitism and ill acquainted with human freedoms. But his encounters with devils and demons were frequent. The destruction of his people by them left an indelible mark on his narrative imagination.

## The Demons of Isaac Bashevis Singer

Isaac Bashevis Singer, one of the most formidable storytellers of our century, incorporated hosts of devils and demons into his writing. But Singer's demonology is a subtle commentary on the human condition, addressing the most lacerating of questions: the meaning (or meaninglessness) of evil, the role (if any) of the Deity in the economy of existence, the nature of reality, the polarities of the struggle within each of us, the confusion between the conceptions of "God" and "Satan," and the thin line between the rational and the psychotic.

Singer's vision of the world is fundamentally bleak. A native of Poland and the son of a Rabbi, he lived most of his life in America. But he was a mature man upon his arrival to these shores, and so had had the opportunity to absorb the Polish Jewish experience. When he writes of Warsaw or Lublin there is no question that the spirit of their characters pours forth from the author's very pores. He knew them as he knew his own brother. When he came to live in New York and write about the American venue he was still writing of what his brother and literary mentor, I. J. Singer, was to call "a world that is no more" (which is also the title of his fine memoir on the experience of his youth). Singer's reactions to the destruction of the three million Jews of Poland, fully half the number of Jews incinerated during the Holocaust Tremendum, are reflected in many of his short stories, which feature demons in a variety of settings. The Holocaust was to Isaac Bashevis Singer the monstrously huge incarnation of an upside-down world, a human society fed on illusions and delusions, utterly incapable of making distinctions between heaven and earth or between Eden and Gehenna.

In "Jachid and Jechidah,"[8] a rebellious female angel, Jechidah, is condemned to death—that is, to life on earth—by the heavenly tribunal for a variety of crimes and misdemeanors, but mostly for unjustly suspecting her angelic lover, Jachid, of infidelity. Dumah, the Angel of Death, arrives to do his job, and Jechidah flies into hysterics at the sight of him. Dumah expostulates with her:

"Jechidah, I know you are angry with me. But is it my fault, sister? Did I want to be the Angel of Death? I too am a sinner, exiled from a higher realm, my punishment to be the executioner of souls. Jechidah, I have not willed your death, but be comforted. Death is not as dreadful as you imagine. True, the first moments are not easy. But once you have been planted in the womb, the nine months that follow are not painful.

"You will forget all that you have learned here. Coming out of the womb will be a shock; but childhood is often pleasant. You will begin to study the lore of death, clothed in a fresh, pliant body, and soon will dread the end of your exile."

Once on earth, Jechidah grows to be a lovely young woman. She meets a medical student named Jachid. Both experience a sense of déjà vu. They fall in love and, in due course, Jechidah becomes pregnant:

They saw a soul condemned to sink down to Earth. Jechidah knew that this soul would become her daughter. Just before she woke up (after a night with Jachid), Jechidah heard a voice: "The grave (her womb) and the grave digger (Jachid's procreating organ) have met. The burial (conception) will take place tonight."

Life and death, the perishable and imperishable, are each turned into the other by Singer. The human womb can be viewed as a tomb, but humankind continues to celebrate birth and to dread death, little comprehending that death is the liberation of the soul.

Singer delights in paradox, in turning ideas on their heads. It is humans, for example, who are typically frightened by demons. But in his story "Shiddah and Kuziba,"[9] it is the other way around. Shiddah, a demon living very deep beneath the earth's surface, tries to comfort her child, Kuziba, who has persistent nightmares about the horrible *Homo sapiens* monster. One day the child's forebodings are realized when the drilling machines of humans come within earshot of the demonic mother and child. They cannot escape to the lower depths since that area is already blocked. So the only out is to rise to the very surface, which is the domain of the human monster. Shiddah explains:

> ". . . up there, there would also be caves, marshes, graves, dark rocky crevices; there, too, she had heard there were dense forests and empty deserts. Man had not covered the whole world with his greed. There, too, lived demons, imps, shades, hobgoblins."

Shiddah and Kuziba would find a provisional haven on earth's surface, pending their final liberation.

> For Shiddah knew that the last victory would be to darkness. Until then, demons who were forsaken or driven out would have to suffer patience. But a time would come when the light of the universe would be extinguished. All the stars

would be snuffed out; all voices silenced; all surfaces cut off. God and Satan would be one. The remembrance of man and his abominations would be nothing but a bad dream which God had spun out for awhile to distract himself in his eternal night.

Singer's abysmal apocalypse, dour as it is, cleaves to a Jewish tradition that harks back to Isaiah: "I form light and create darkness. I make weal and create woe—I the Lord do all these things." It is in this sense that one must take the sentence "God and Satan would be one." With the disappearance of humanity, there remains no function for Satan, God's alter-ego, in the domain of the evil that men do. The divine experiment with the creation of Adam and Eve will have failed, undone by man's freedom to choose between life and death. The choice having been made, once again "the rest is silence," the silence of eternal night.

The theme of hopelessness in the wake of the fires of the crematoria is at its most devastating in "The Last Demon,"[10] also by Singer. It begins:

> "I, a demon, bear witness that there are no more demons left. Why demons, when man himself is a demon? Why persuade to evil someone who is already convinced? I am the last of the persuaders."

This nameless demon is sent to work in the one-horse town of Tishevitz. But he soon discovers that there is no work to be done there. A languishing demon in the shape of a spider tells the new arrival that he has been spinning his wheels instead of his webs for over two hundred years. There simply is no one left to ensnare. Tishevitz was a graveyard. A solitary Jew is the surviving symbol of the decay and evanescence of a once vital center of Jewish piety and learning. He is a Rabbi without a congregation, a teacher without students. He is left with his Talmud, which he pores over day and night, communing with himself and with his God—an unassailable target to the last demon. With nothing to do, the demon is desperate to go elsewhere and seek some action. But an order comes to him from Asmodeus, the Prince of Demons: "Stay in Tishevitz (read Auschwitz) and fry." The last demon muses bitterly:

"How long am I here? Eternity plus a Wednesday. I've seen it all, the destruction of Tishevitz, the destruction of Poland. There are no more Jews, no more demons. The women don't pour out water any longer on the night of the winter solstice. They don't avoid giving things in even numbers. They no longer knock at dawn at the antechamber of the synagogue. They don't warn us before emptying the slops.[11] The Rabbi was martyred on a Friday in the month of Nisan. The community was slaughtered, the holy books burned, the cemetery desecrated . . . There is no longer an Angel of Good nor an Angel of Evil. No more sins, no more temptations! The generation is already guilty seven times over, but Messiah does not come. To whom should he come? Messiah did not come to the Jews, so the Jews went to Messiah. There is no further need for demons. We have also been annihilated. I am the last, a refugee. I can go any-where I please, but where should a demon like me go, to the murderers?"

A solitary book of Yiddish stories still survives, hidden between two broken barrels in the house that once be-longed to Velvel the Barrelmaker (Singer himself?). The demon finds it to be gibberish, though the book's moral is that there exists neither judge nor justice. Says the demon:

> "As long as a single volume remains, I have something to sustain me. As long as the moths have not destroyed the last page, there is something to play with . . . When the last letter is gone, the last of the demons is done."

The fires of the Nazi *Gehenna* rage through many of Isaac Bashevis Singer's stories. He has no ready answers to the questions raised by the Holocaust. The closest he comes to "explaining" it is to suggest in a variety of contexts that Satan had displaced God. It is not surprising that, as was the case in the previous story, the teller of the tale "The Destruction of Kreshev"[12] is of Satan and Company—in-deed, he's the "headman" himself. The narrative is about an aberrant marriage. A lovely young woman weds a wildly eccentric man who turns out to be a secret follower of the long-since-dead false Messiah, Sabbetai Zvi. In imi-tation of his master's penchant for descent into the bowels of abominations as a means for hastening the Redemption, the husband encourages his wife to enter into an adulterous relationship with his handsome, cynical, and nihilistic coachman. When this abomination becomes public the outrage of the Jewish community is vented upon all three of the perpetrators. The wife is driven to hang herself. The husband, repentant, begins to pine away through self-flagellation and fasting. The coachman disappears. A short time after these events, the town of Kreshev is incinerated by a fire of mysterious origin.

Sabbatianism serves Singer well as a vehicle to convey the dominion of evil in a world gone insane. The blandishments of Shloimele, the husband, upon his wife, Lise, are an encapsulation of the teaching of evil as religion and the conflagration that must follow if such a religion entices enough followers.

Singer presents us with a world in which good and evil have become devoid of meaning. "I love fire!" Shloimele exclaims. "I love a holocaust. I would like the whole world to burn and Asmodeus to take over the rule." This bleak post-Auschwitz eschatology doesn't necessarily reflect the spirit of Judaism or the beliefs of Singer himself.

About fifteen years ago, Singer appeared at a public lecture in my community of Kansas City, Missouri. I had the privilege of introducing him to the audience. He spoke in his simple, unassuming, but very effective style, and I took notes of what he said because I was also to serve as moderator of a panel discussion immediately following his talk. Here are the pertinent words:

"You ask about God? I haven't made personal contact with Him lately. Either He's been avoiding me, or maybe I've been avoiding Him. When I was a boy, I talked to Him a lot. And I even thought I heard Him answer from time to time. But in the last thirty, forty years He seems to have given over His work to incompetent, even evil, people. I can't believe that He would allow our eyes to see what we saw or our ears to hear what we heard. I live in the hope that He will be back where we want Him to be. But maybe we should let Him know about it."

This last thought is reminiscent of the Hasidic master's assurance that God is "wherever we invite Him to be." If humankind elects to banish the godly, we create a vacuum that is soon filled by the demonic. If it's angels we want, they are at hand. If it's devils we crave, we will be engulfed by them. The spirit of Judaism emphatically rejects the inevitability of disaster. It has never accepted the sovereignty of evil as "necessary." On the contrary, for over three thousand years Judaism has pronounced the mission of humankind as the remodeling of the world after the pattern of God's Kingdom, a realm in which truth, compassion, and justice prevail.

All of that takes mighty effort. But all of that is the purpose of human life.

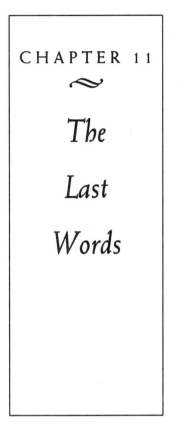

CHAPTER 11

*The*

*Last*

*Words*

~ ~ ~ ~ ~ ~ ~ ~ ~ ~ ~ ~ ~ ~ ~ ~ ~ ~ ~ ~ ~ ~ ~ ~ ~

The last words of prophecy in the Hebrew Bible read:

> Lo, I will send the prophet Elijah to you before the coming
> of the awesome, fearful day of the Lord. He shall reconcile

fathers with sons and sons with their fathers, so that, when I come, I do not strike the whole land with utter destruction.

(MALACHI 3:23, 24)

The survival of the human race is dependent upon reconciliation. Elijah the *prophet*, not Elijah the angel—earthly man, not celestial being—must become God's instrument for the redemption of humanity. Reliance upon the supernatural as the source for salvation has been a snare and a delusion throughout recorded history. It has also been an excuse for letting things stay just the way they are. Worse, it has been the byword of the oppressors through the ages: "It is the will of God," they have said. "Let suffering be suffered."

But it cannot be that God wills suffering. We would not worship a God of that sort. The Hebrew Bible sees God in a different light, for His first words were: "Let there be light" and His first question to man was: "Where are you hiding?" The question was a terrible accusation that Adam and Eve were trying to escape their responsibilities. God's second question, to Cain, the killer, still reverberates in His universe: "What have you done? Hark, your brother's blood cries out to Me from the ground!"

At the very beginning of the peoplehood of Israel, by the shores of the Red Sea, with the Egyptians in pursuit close behind, Moses frantically looks heavenward for guidance. That guidance comes immediately with the Lord's words: "Why do you cry out to Me? Tell the Israelites to go forward!" Human action must be antecedent to any miracles that might lie in store. Man is not helpless, for the divine is within him. His mission on earth is to activate it—to create, build, and nurture. This is what the Rabbis of the Talmud meant in saying: "God designed man as His partner in the work of the Creation." Even the angels had to understand that God treasured humanity above all, even above them. The Midrash relates that when the Israelites crossed the Red Sea safely, leaving hordes of Egyptians flailing about in the waters, the angels began to sing to God a paean of praise. He immediately reproved them, saying, "The creatures of My hand are drowning. Is this a time for song?" There are no victories and no celebrations when corpses, even those of the "enemy," lie strewn over the landscape or seascape.

The archetype of all Jewish angels, the Archangel Michael, is guardian and lifesaver through all of the Rabbinic literature. He rescues Abraham from the fires of Nimrod. He protects Sarah from being defiled by Abimelech. He saves Lot from a Sodom in flames. He rescues Jacob from the threatening clutches of his brother, Esau. He prevents Laban from carrying out his design to harm Jacob. He snatches Tamar from the stake. He shields Shadrach, Meshach, and Abednego from Nebuchadnezzar's searing furnace. He confutes Haman's accusations against the Jews in the domains of Ahaseurus. And, at the end of humanity's long trail of tribulations, Michael will defeat Samael-Satan in mortal combat, thus relegating the symbol of evil to oblivion.

Michael is the heavenly model of what man should be, what man *can* be. Millions of angels were engendered by the imagination of Jewish writers during ancient and medieval times. Hundreds of them were assigned specific tasks by their human creators. But of the entire "gathering of angels" only the Archangel Michael was designated as the Prince of Israel, the special guardian and role model of the Jewish people. In Isaiah 29, Ariel is a synonym for the city of Jerusalem, Michael's special charge:

> Ah, Ariel, Ariel
> City where David camped!
> . . . . . . . . . . . . . . . . . .
> And like fine dust shall be
> The multitude of your strangers
> And like flying chaff
> The multitude of tyrants.
> And suddenly, in an instant,
> She shall be remembered of the Lord of Hosts
> With roaring and shaking and deafening noise,
> Storm, and tempest, and blaze of consuming fire.

For Jerusalem, the "city of peace," is the natural habitat of the angel of peace. Michael's wings flutter over the city of David awaiting the day when Ariel will be released from the fratricidal strife of millennia and when the vision of Isaiah's second chapter will be realized:

In the days to come
The Mount of the Lord's House
Shall stand firm above the mountains
And tower above the hills;
And all the nations
Shall gaze on it with joy.
And the many peoples shall go and say:
"Come, let us go up to the Mount of the Lord,
To the House of the God of Jacob;
That He may instruct us in His ways,
And that we may walk in His paths."
For instruction shall come forth from Zion,
The word of the Lord from Jerusalem.
Thus He will judge among the nations
And arbitrate for many peoples,
And they shall beat their swords into ploughshares
And their spears into pruning hooks:
Nation shall not take up sword against nation,
They shall never again know war.

IN 1929, ARABS FIRED GUNS into the then-new suburb of Jerusalem, Kiryat Moshe, where my parents had built a home for the family. Since we were within the range of the snipers, an official of the community came to our house and ordered us out of the line of fire into the interior of Kiryat Moshe. We all ran in panic, including my paternal grandmother, who, grabbing my hand, had begun to recite the Ninety-first Psalm. She gasped the words:

> "I say of the Lord, my refuge and stronghold,
> My God in whom I trust
> That He will save you from the fowler's trap,
> From the destructive plague . . .
> You need not fear the terror by night,
> or the arrow that flies by day,
> The plague that stalks in the darkness,
> or the scourge that ravages at noon . . .
> No harm will befall you,
> No disease will touch your tent,
> For He will order His angels
> to guard you wherever you go.
> They will carry you in their hands
> lest you stumble on a rock . . ."

# Endnotes

Chapter Three ≈ ≈ ≈ ≈ ≈ ≈ ≈ ≈ ≈ ≈ ≈ ≈ ≈ ≈ ≈ ≈ ≈

1. T. H. Gaster, *The Dead Sea Scriptures* (Garden City, N.Y.: Doubleday & Co., 1956), pp. 43–44.
2. Edgar A. Poe, "The Raven."
3. Gaster, *The Dead Sea Scriptures*, pp. 44–45.
4. J. H. Charlesworth, *The Old Testament Pseudepigrapha*, vol. 1 (Garden City, N.Y.: Doubleday & Co., 1990).
5. Ibid.
6. Ibid.
7. E. J. Goodspeed, *The Apocrypha* (New York, N.Y.: Random House, 1959), p. 113. Jewish law requires the nearest of kin to marry a childless widow.
8. Ibid., p. 117.
9. Ibid., pp. 126–127.

10. Charlesworth, *Old Testament Pseudepigrapha*.
11. Ibid.
12. Ibid.
13. Ibid.
14. Ibid.

## Chapter Four ≈ ≈ ≈ ≈ ≈ ≈ ≈ ≈ ≈ ≈ ≈ ≈ ≈ ≈ ≈ ≈

1. The name Jared means "he who descended."
2. The Hebrew *Hermon* derives from *Herem*, which means curse or bar.
3. Charlesworth, *Old Testament Pseudepigrapha*.
4. Ibid.
5. Ibid.
6. Ibid. Precisely the belief of the Scroll people (see chapter 3).
7. Louis Ginzberg, *The Legends of the Jews* (Philadelphia, Pa.: Jewish Publication Society, 1946), vol. 4, p. 115. This monumental seven-volume opus is the source used throughout for the translation of the Midrashic materials in this chapter as well as in other chapters throughout.
8. Moses Gaster, *Ma'aseh Book* (Philadelphia, Pa.: Jewish Publication Society, 1934), vol. 1, p. 30.
9. Ibid., vol. 3, p. 120.

## Chapter Five ≈ ≈ ≈ ≈ ≈ ≈ ≈ ≈ ≈ ≈ ≈ ≈ ≈ ≈ ≈ ≈

1. It is more than a bibliophile's footnote to mention that one of America's giant publishing enterprises, Random House, is in

the process of printing an English version of *The Talmud: The Steinsaltz Edition*, 6 volumes of which have appeared to date. It may be added that if the full project is carried through, it will take perhaps 150 volumes to encompass it.

2. Ginzberg, *The Legends of the Jews*, vol. 1, p. 201.

3. A. Jellinek, *Bet Hamidrash* (Jerusalem, 1938). This book is written in Hebrew. Author's translation.


## Chapter Six ≈ ≈ ≈ ≈ ≈ ≈ ≈ ≈ ≈ ≈ ≈ ≈ ≈ ≈ ≈

1. Joshua Trachtenberg, *Jewish Magic and Superstition* (Philadelphia, Pa.: Jewish Publication Society, 1939).

2. Ginzberg, *The Legends of the Jews*, vol. 4, pp. 168–69.

3. Bernard Bemberger, *Fallen Angels* (Philadelphia, Pa.: Jewish Publication Society, 1952).

4. Gershom Scholem, *Kabbalah* (New York, N.Y.: Quadrangle/New York Times Book Co., 1974), pp. 358–59.


## Chapter Seven ≈ ≈ ≈ ≈ ≈ ≈ ≈ ≈ ≈ ≈ ≈ ≈ ≈ ≈ ≈

1. This and the Hasidic tales that follow are drawn from Louis I. Newman, *The Hasidic Anthology* (New York, N.Y.: Bloch Publishing Company, 1944).


## Chapter Eight ≈ ≈ ≈ ≈ ≈ ≈ ≈ ≈ ≈ ≈ ≈ ≈ ≈ ≈ ≈

1. Ginzberg, *The Legends of the Jews*.

## Chapter Ten ∽ ∽ ∽ ∽ ∽ ∽ ∽ ∽ ∽ ∽ ∽ ∽ ∽ ∽ ∽

1. Adin Steinsaltz, *The Thirteen Petalled Rose* (Northvale, N.J.: Jason Aronson, 1980).
2. Robert Alter, *Necessary Angels* (Cambridge, Mass.: Harvard University Press, 1991; in association with Hebrew Union College Press, Cincinnati).
3. Nachman Rupp, "The Eden Angel," in Howard Schwartz, ed. *Gates to the New City* (New York, N.Y.: Avon Books, 1981).
4. Martin Buber, "The Angel and the World's Dominion," in Schwartz, ed. *Gates to the New City.*
5. Howard Schwartz, "The Three Souls of Reb Anaron," in Schwartz, ed., *Gates to the New City.*
6. Isaac Leib Peretz, "Silent Bontche," in *Prince of the Ghetto,* trans. Maurice Samuel (Philadelphia, Pa.: Jewish Publication Society, 1959).
7. Martin Gilbert, *The Holocaust* (New York, N.Y.: Holt, Rinehart and Winston, 1985), pp. 581–82.
8. Isaac Bashevis Singer, "Jachid and Jechidah," in *Short Friday* (Philadelphia, Pa.: Jewish Publication Society, 1965).
9. Isaac Bashevis Singer, "Shidah and Kuziba," in *The Spinoza of Market Street* (Philadelphia, Pa.: Jewish Publication Society, 1961).
10. Singer, "The Last Demon," in *Short Friday.*
11. These are superstitious practices designed to ward off demons.
12. Singer, "The Destruction of Kreshev," in *The Spinoza of Market Street.*

# Bibliography

Agnon, Shmel Yosef. *Days of Awe*. (Hebrew) Jerusalem & New York: Schocken, 1947

Almog, Samuel, ed. *Anti-Semitism Through the Ages*. New York: Pergamon Press, 1988

Alter, R. *The Art of Biblical Narrative*. New York: Basic Books, 1981

———. *Necessary Angels*. Cambridge: Harvard University Press, 1991

Avigad, N. and Yadin, Y. *A Genesis Apocryphon: A Scroll from the Wilderness of Judaea*. Jerusalem: Magnes Press, 1956

Baer, Yitzhak. *A History of the Jews in Christian Spain*. 2 vols. Philadelphia: Jewish Publication Society, 1961

Bamberger, Bernard. *Fallen Angels*. Philadelphia: Jewish Publication Society, 1956

Baron, Salo W. *A Social and Religious History of the Jews*. 18 vols. Philadelphia: Jewish Publication Society, 1952–1983

Ben-Sasson, H. H., ed. *A History of the Jewish People*. Cambridge: Harvard University Press, 1976

*Biblical Encyclopedia*. Hebrew language ed. 8 vols., Jerusalem: 1950–1982

Braude, William and Kapstein, Israel. *Pesikta de-Rab Kahana*. Philadelphia: Jewish Publication Society, 1985

———. *Tanna Debe Eliyahu*. Philadelphia: Jewish Publication Society, 1981

Buber, Martin. *Tales of the Hassidim*. Hebrew. Tel Aviv: Schocken, 1957

Carmi, T., ed. *The Penguin Book of Hebrew Verse*. New York: Viking, 1981

Charlesworth, James H. *The Old Testament Pseudepigrapha*. 2 vols. New York: Doubleday, 1988

Cohen, Arthur. *The Myth of the Judeo-Christian Tradition*. New York: Harper & Row, 1957

Davidson, G. *A Dictionary of Angels*. New York: Free Press, 1967

Dawidowicz, Lucy. *The War Against the Jews: 1933–1945*. New York: Holt, Rinehart & Winston, 1975

Donin, Hayim, *To Pray as a Jew*. New York: Basic Books, 1980

Dubnow, Simon. *History of Hasidism*. Hebrew language ed. Tel Aviv: Dvir, 1944

———. *History of the Jews in Russia and Poland*. 3 vols. Philadelphia: Jewish Publication Society, 1916

Dunham, Barrows. *Heroes and Heretics*. New York: Alfred Knopf, 1964

Dupont-Sommer, A. *The Jewish Sect of Qumran and the Essenes*. New York: Macmillan, 1955

Epstein, I., ed. *The Soncino Talmud*. 18 vols.

Frazer, James G. *The Golden Bough*. New York: Macmillan, 1940

Gaster, Moses. *Ma'Aseh Book*. 2 vols. Philadelphia: Jewish Publication Society, 1934

Gaster, Theodore. *The Dead Sea Scriptures in English Translation*. New York: Doubleday, 1956

Gilbert, Martin. *The Holocaust*. New York: Holt, Rinehart & Winston, 1985

Ginzberg, Louis. *The Legends of the Jews*. 7 vols. Philadelphia: Jewish Publication Society, 1946

Goodspeed, Edgar J. *The Apocrypha: An American Translation*. New York: Random House, 1959

Hilberg, Raoul. *The Destruction of European Jewry*. New York: Harper & Row, 1979

Hooke, S. H. *Middle Eastern Mythology*. Baltimore: Penguin Books, 1963

Ibn-Shmuel, Yehudah. *Midrashei Geulah*. Hebrew language ed. Tel Aviv: Mossad Bialik, 1954

Jellinek, A. *Bet ha-Midrash*. Hebrew language ed. 6 vols. Jerusalem: Bamberger-Wahrman, 1938

Jewish Publication Society, ed. *The Bible: A New Translation*. Philadelphia: Jewish Publication Society, 1982

Katz, J. *From Prejudice to Destruction*. Cambridge: Harvard University Press, 1980

Kaufmann, Yehezkel. *The Religion of Israel*. Translated and abridged from the Hebrew by Moshe Greenberg. Chicago: University of Chicago Press, 1960

Kramer, S. N., ed. *Mythologies of the Ancient World*. Garden City: Doubleday, 1961

Lacks, Roslyn. *Women and Judaism*. New York: Doubleday, 1980

Laqueur, Walter. *The Terrible Secret*. Boston: Little, Brown & Co., 1980

Lauterbach, Jacob Z. *Mekilta de-Rabbi Ishmael*. 3 vols. Philadelphia: Jewish Publication Society, 1949

Levi, Primo. *Survival in Auschwitz*. New York: Collier Books, 1953

Lifton, R. J. *The Nazi Doctors*. New York: Basic Books, 1986

Maimonides, Moses. *A Guide to the Perplexed*. New York: Hebrew Publishing Co., 1881

Margolies, Morris B. *Torah-Vision*. New York: Phillip Feldheim, 1961

Margolies, Reuven, ed. *Sefer Hasidim*. Hebrew language ed. Jerusalem: Mossad Harav Kook, 1957

Margolis, Max. *The Hebrew Scriptures in the Making*. Philadelphia: Jewish Publication Society, 1948

Millgram, Abraham. *Jewish Worship*. Philadelphia: Jewish Publication Society, 1971

Montefiore, C. G. and Loewe, H. *A Rabbinic Anthology*. Philadelphia: Jewish Publication Society, 1960

Newman, Louis I. *The Hasidic Anthology*. New York: Bloch Publishing Co., 1944

Pearl, C. *Rashi (Rabbi Solomon Ben Isaac)*. New York: Viking, 1970

Poliakov, L. *The History of Anti-Semitism*. 5 vols. New York: Vanguard Press, 1945

Reitlinger, Gerald. *The Final Solution*. New York: A. S. Barnes & Co., 1953

Samuel, Maurice. *Prince of the Ghetto*. Philadelphia: Jewish Publication Society, 1959

Sarachek, Joseph. *The Doctrine of the Messiah in Medieval Jewish Literature*. New York: Hermon Press, 1968

Sarna, N. *Understanding Genesis*. New York: McGraw-Hill, 1966

Schechter, Solomon. *Some Aspects of Rabbinic Theology*. New York: Behrman House, 1936

Scholem, Gershom. *Major Trends in Jewish Mysticism*. New York: Schocken Books, 1941

———. *Sabbetai Sevi, the Mystical Messiah*. Princeton: Princeton University Press, 1973

Shaked, S. "Some Notes on Ahreman, The Evil Spirit, and His Creation." In *Studies in Mysticism and Religion Presented to Gershom G. Scholem*. Jerusalem: Magres Press, 1967

Singer, I. B. *Satan in Goray*. New York: Noonday Press, 1955

Smith, Homer W. *Man and His Gods*. New York: Grosset & Dunlap, 1952

Spiegel, Shalom. *The Last Trial*. Philadelphia: Jewish Publication Society, 1967

Steinberg, M. *Basic Judaism*. New York: Harcourt-Brace, 1947

Steinsaltz, A. *The Essential Talmud*. New York: Basic Books, 1976

Tishby, I., ed. *The Wisdom of the Zohar*. 2 vols. (Hebrew), Jerusalem: Mossad Bialik, 1957

Trachtenberg, Joshua. *The Devil and the Jews*. Philadelphia: Jewish Publication Society, 1961

———. *Jewish Magic and Superstition.* New York: Meridian, 1961

Underhill, Evelyn. *Mysticism*, 12 ed. London: Methuen, 1930

Urbach, Ephraim. *The Sages: Their Concepts and Beliefs.* (Hebrew). Jerusalem: Magnes Press, 1969

Vermes, G. *The Dead Sea Scrolls: Qumran in Perspective.* Cleveland: Collins & World, 1978

Waxman, M. *A History of Jewish Literature.* 6 vols. New York: Thomas Yoseloff, 1960

Wiesel, Elie. *Souls on Fire.* New York: Random House, 1972

Wilson, Edmund. *The Dead Sea Scrolls.* New York: Oxford University Press, 1969

Wyman, David S. *The Abandonment of the Jews.* New York: Pantheon Books, 1984

Yadin, Y. *The Message of the Scrolls.* New York: Grosset & Dunlap, 1968

———. *War of the Sons of Light Against the Sons of Darkness.* Hebrew language ed. Jerusalem: Mossad Bialik, 1955

Yahil, Leni. *The Holocaust.* New York: Oxford University Press, 1990.

## About the Author

MORRIS B. MARGOLIES, a rabbi for forty-three years, is now a professor of Jewish History at the University of Kansas. He is the author of scholarly books and articles. He lives in Kansas with his wife of forty-two years.